WILLIAMS-SONOMA

two in the kitchen

CHRISTIE DUFAULT and JORDAN MACKAY

PHOTOGRAPHS by KATE SEARS

weldonowen

a note from

CHRISTIE and JORDAN

We met in what, given who we are, was the most natural way possible: at work and in a restaurant. Christie was the wine director for one of San Francisco's top restaurants, and Jordan was the wine writer for one of the city magazines, covering a story about local sommeliers. Of all of the many sommeliers Jordan interviewed, Christie was the only one who offered a glass of Champagne. It was the brut rosé of H. Billiot Fils, and a decade later we still drink it with sentimentality.

Now married for five years, wine and food continue to be at the center of our lives and our relationship. Today, Christie teaches about wine full-time at the Culinary Institute of America in Napa Valley, and Jordan continues to write about the grand universe of food, wine, and spirits. Although our jobs provide us regular access to the efforts of the world's best chefs, bartenders, and winemakers, what gives us the most joy is mixing a drink or uncorking a wine and cooking at home together.

We both grew up in households in which family mealtime was sacred, and the rituals surrounding eating and drinking have continued to define and unite us. Today, we always start by setting a beautiful table—cloth napkins, proper wineglasses—and carry that same attentiveness through the execution of the menu. Whether it's a simple dinner for two in the kitchen, an alfresco brunch for friends, or a holiday feast in the dining room, we honor the meal by creating a welcoming setting and cooking food from the heart. It's our way of reveling in each other and in our union. We hope that you will find the same bliss in the kitchen that we do.

Christie Dufault   *Jordan Mackay*

CONTRIBUTING COUPLES

JULIE and MATT WALKER

The owners of the creative studio Tiger in a Jar (www.tigerinajar.com) in Salt Lake City, UT, Julie and Matt specialize in film and creative craft projects, and exploring new ways to make things less ordinary. They spend most of their free time obsessing about food.

SAUKOK and JAMIE TIAMPO

A trained chef and photographer, Jamie owns SeeFood Media, a kitchen studio specializing in food-focused TV and web video production. Saukok owns 57Grand, a weddingwear collection inspired by New York, and REVEL, a shop-able inspiration site for modern celebrations.

MINDY SEGAL and DAN THOMPKINS

A James Beard–nominated pastry chef, Mindy is the owner of HotChocolate Restaurant and Dessert Bar in Chicago. Her writing has been featured in numerous national publications. In their free time, Mindy and Dan can be found searching for antiques or drinking craft beer all over the world.

AKI KAMOZAWA and ALEX TALBOT

As the co-owners of Ideas in Food (www.ideasinfood.com)—a book, a blog, and a consulting business based in Levittown, PA—Aki and Alex offer chefs and other food professionals tailored workshops on modern culinary techniques, photography, and writing.

ANDREA REUSING and MAC MCCAUGHAN

Andrea is the chef and owner of Lantern in Chapel Hill, NC and is the author of *Cooking in the Moment: A Year of Seasonal Recipes.* Mac plays music with Superchunk and Portastatic and is the co-founder of the independent record label Merge Records.

MOLLY WIZENBERG and BRANDON PETTIT

In 2009, Molly and Brandon opened the restaurant Delancey in Seattle. Brandon is the chef. Molly created Orangette (www.orangette.net), named the best food blog in the world by the *London Times,* and her first book was a *New York Times* bestseller.

LISA and EMMETT FOX

After several years in Boston heading up a catering company and different kitchens, Lisa and Emmett moved to Austin and opened ASTI Trattoria and FINO Restaurant Patio & Bar. Both spots reflect their continued passion for travel and culinary adventure.

CONTENTS

TWO COOKS *in the* KITCHEN

When we talk of cooking together, it's not about doing every task with both pairs of hands. Instead, it's about jointly producing a great meal, whether it's just for us or for a tableful of guests. Regardless of the size of the party, our mantra is the same: divide and conquer. In other words, we divvy up the various tasks and promise to meet at the end.

Our cooking together starts with strategizing. We come up with a general menu, and then usually choose to take ownership of different courses. A single shopping list is drawn up, and, typically, one of us goes to the market with the big list while the other one stays home and begins prepping what we already have on hand.

We like recipes, but we also like to deviate from them. A great benefit of cooking together is that one of us always seems to have a good idea of what can be left out or what can be added to a recipe, so we continually share thoughts as we plan and work on our respective dishes. One thing we have learned, and you should too, is to read a recipe through from beginning to end before you start cooking. If you don't, it's easy to get caught unprepared.

THE IMPORTANCE OF PREP

Great preperation is essential. Just like on cooking shows, you'll want to measure, chop, and separate all of your ingredients before you start to cook. It reduces stress, the kitchen stays neater, and the food always comes out better. We find it useful to have a bunch of bowls in graduated sizes to contain prepped ingredients until it's time to use them.

We're all about "clean as you go," too. We don't leave carrot peels and garlic skins lying around on the counter. We wipe our work surface clean after each step. Having on hand a good supply of clean dish towels (way more than you think you'll ever need) is very helpful so we can use them with abandon.

Communication is key. Even though we work on separate tasks, plenty of banter fills the kitchen. Does this look done? Are these chopped finely enough? Does this need more salt? We respect each other's palates, so our nearly continuous conversation makes each dish a friendly collaboration.

Nothing is more dispiriting than a messy kitchen, so we make it our goal to return it to pristine cleanliness before we go to bed. (Of course, whether this happens or not depends on how late the dinner ran and how much wine was consumed.) Just as with the cooking, cleaning up is a joint effort. One of us might scrub the pan while the other wipes down the table and blows out the candles. And when everything is done and the last dish towel is hung up to dry, that's when we know we've conquered the mess.

KITCHEN CONFIDENCE

If you are new to cooking and want to get more comfortable in the kitchen, try preparing one cooked dish at a time. Take turns choosing a dish or focus on one cuisine and select different recipes to sample. You can round out any meal with some good bread and a simple green salad. The more at ease you are cooking for yourselves, the more relaxed you'll be cooking for others.

MAKING WEEKNIGHT COOKING FUN

If both of you have had long days, you don't want making dinner to seem like a chore. Here are ways to make it fun:

Try new things. Too much routine can seem like drudgery. Challenge yourselves by cooking recipes you've never made before.

Fire up the grill. Even on cold days, a little fire and smoke in the backyard or on a balcony can raise tired spirits.

Host your own cooking competition. Go to the store, buy a random set of ingredients, and challenge your spouse to create a meal. Swap roles the next week.

Honor the dinner table. Don't get too deep into the habit of watching TV programs or movies during dinners. Instead, cook together and then enjoy the meal at the table with wine and candlelight.

Le Diner du Soleil

Aperitif

Shaved Zucchini
Salad

Herb-Roasted
Pork Loin

Plateau Fromage

Grilled Plums

ENTERTAINING *as a* COUPLE

We entertain a lot because creating a meal together, and then sharing it with others, is fun. When it all goes well, and you work as a team, the feeling that we've given our friends a memorable evening, and had a great time in the process, is addictive.

So if you're going to the effort and expense of entertaining, make it memorable. How do you do that? One thing we do is write the menu and the date on a chalkboard and post it in the dining room, an easy-to-do touch that our guests love. We also snap a photo of each meal for our scrapbook.

We like to create themes, too. For example, sometimes we'll borrow an Iron Chef format, in which each course must use the same ingredient. Other times we'll plan a dinner around a specific wine region that we love, such as Tuscany. Or, we may go out of our way to showcase a special seasonal ingredient, such as oysters from up the coast or a high-end cut of meat.

But dinner parties should be memorable for the hosts, as well, and that means it helps to put in time planning the get-together. Nothing is more disappointing than throwing a brilliant dinner party and discovering at the end of the evening that you worked so hard that you didn't enjoy yourself. Being well prepared, and then going with the flow, is the best way to guarantee your own enjoyment.

THE WELL-STOCKED BAR

Gin: One bottle of a good, versatile gin like Plymouth or Beefeater.

Whiskey: Up to three kinds are ideal: bourbon, blended scotch, and single-malt scotch.

Vodka: Any mid-range variety will work.

Campari: The world's greatest aperitif.

Tequila: A nice blanco, such as El Tesoro.

Rum: A basic dark rum can be used in many different cocktails.

Brandy: A decent Cognac or Armagnac is useful for both drinking and cooking.

Vermouth: Keep one half-bottle of sweet and one half-bottle of dry in the fridge.

Cointreau: An orange-flavored liqueur that's essential to many cocktails, from the margarita to the sidecar to the cosmopolitan.

Amaro: A bitter Italian digestif like Ramazzotti, Fernet-Branca, or Averna is handy in helping to settle a big meal.

SETTING UP A HOME BAR

Whether it is just some bottles on a tray in the corner, or a cabinet shelf or several devoted to your favorite liquors, a smartly stocked bar comes in handy for entertaining. Sometimes a potent cocktail or a sip of something strong fits the bill better than wine or beer can, and it's nice to be able to give guests just what they want.

Luckily, as far as ingredients go, a functional bar is easy to put together and only a handful of tools are necessary. First, you'll need a shaker, of which there are two basic kinds: the cobbler and the Boston. The former is all metal and has a tumbler, a tight lid, and a built-in strainer. The latter, which we prefer (the lid can be difficult to get off the cobbler when it is cold), combines a pint-glass tumbler and a metal tumbler that fit together. If you opt for a Boston, you'll need a Hawthorne strainer, one of those perforated steel paddles with the spring around it that fits nice and tight. You'll also need a long spoon for stirring in a shaker or pitcher, and a jigger (usually ½ ounce/15 ml on one side and 1 ounce/30 ml on the other) for measuring. A citrus press comes in handy, as does a zester for making twists.

Ideally, your bar setup will have a practical assortment of glassware, too. It should include martini glasses (for any chilled drinks without ice); short, broad rocks glasses (for mixed drinks served over ice or straight liquor served with or without ice); and tall highball glasses (for drinks made with a carbonated mixer served over ice). If you like a good Tom Collins every now and again, tall, narrow Collins glasses are nice to have (they are good for mojitos and other mixed drinks, too). So, too, are small glasses for serving an amaro or other digestive.

But the true test of a bar is the liquor. If you're after a complete home bar, we've given you a list for the essential spirits here; if this exceeds your space or interest, pare it down. Or, if you want to expand it, consider carrying different styles of gin, a broader selection of whiskeys, such as rye, and a reposado tequila.

To round out the offerings, keep small bottles of soda water and tonic under the bar or in the pantry. Add wine and beer (see pages 237–238), and you'll be well outfitted for any occasion.

CHECKLIST FOR A GREAT DINNER PARTY

*What makes a dinner party successful will vary with each couple, and we encourage
you to work together to create and finesse your signature formula for entertaining.
Here are some considerations and components that help us host our best gatherings.*

PICK THE OCCASION Consider who is coming and why. Will it be a festive get-together or an evening of long, philosophical conversation? Plan the food, drinks, and music accordingly.

DECIDE ON THE MENU Dinner parties are great opportunities to attempt the more ambitious projects you've been saving. That said, you don't want to try anything that you are not certain you can pull off, as nothing is worse than feeling overwhelmed on the food front. We plan an inspired menu that we are confident we can handle and enjoy the party at the same time.

CONSIDER THE SEASONS Gazpacho is never satisfying in winter, and braised short ribs are too heavy for a hot August day. In summer, incorporate the outdoors, such as grilling in the back yard or serving cocktails on a balcony. In winter, serve hearty dishes and warm drinks.

DO WHAT YOU CAN IN ADVANCE Try to ready as much as possible, even a day or two beforehand. Make sauces or soups, wash lettuces and vegetables, and even brown meat that can be finished in the oven just before serving.

PLAN THE SEATING After we were married, we learned a handy rule from the French: Couples should be seated together while they're engaged and for the first year of their marriage. When those twelve months are up, separate them to mix it up and converse or flirt with others.

SERVE HORS D'OEUVRES AND DRINKS A good hour of nibbling and drinking before dinner allows everyone to get comfortable and heightens excitement about the meal to come. Offer cocktails, wine, and beer, and set out an array of light bites, such as olives, nuts, and cured meats (we usually save the cheese for just before dessert, French style).

CLEAR THE TABLE WITH CLASS Treat the clearing of the table in the same way as the staff at a fine restaurant: do not begin removing the dinner plates until the last person has finished.

CHOOSE AND HANDLE WINES WITH CARE Pick out wines that go with the meal. In other words, don't just grab your favorites—select ones that complement the food. Decant those that need decanting, and open all bottles before serving the food. The right wine should be in the glasses before the food comes, not after.

PICK YOUR SERVING STYLE Should you plate the courses or serve them family style? That's the eternal question. For more elegant meals and ones that that require saucing, we usually compose the plates in the kitchen and bring them to the table. But for casual gatherings, we like to set platters on the table and let guests help themselves. Have plenty of nice bowls and platters of varying shapes and sizes for serving.

THINK OF MUSIC AS ANOTHER COURSE Great music is essential to a great dinner party. We generally program one of our computers to play all evening. We think seasonally, choosing contemplative jazz in fall and winter. In summer and spring, we prefer peppier music, like soft indie rock, bright pop music, upbeat jazz, and classic country. Finding the right volume is hard to do. Ideally, it's loud enough to notice, but not so loud that anyone has to shout.

1

BREAKFAST and BRUNCH

BREAKFAST and BRUNCH

*It's amazing how much our lives revolve around
the simple but miraculous little brown farm egg,
a dozen of which is our standard weekly purchase.*

Christie Saturday morning means it's time to ride. We set out early
for the farmers' market, knowing that a noontime brunch will follow.
From our house, we can bike to two markets: the glamorous downtown
market, or the down-home, budget-friendly market. We choose
the market based on how our wallets are feeling.

Jordan Given my job, my love for the cocktail transcends any notion
of the cocktail hour. That means that when we come home from the
market, I can't resist cracking an egg for a wispy Ramos fizz or pisco
sour. The fresher the egg white the frothier the foam.

Christie What to cook for brunch? We've got fresh brown eggs, so
an omelet or frittata is a must. Potatoes? A quick boil and then a
sauté until brown. Mushrooms, kale, broccoli—whatever we carried
home—along with herbs and goat cheese, are folded into the eggs.

Jordan Cooking with an airy cocktail in hand is only civilized. Yes,
a drink before noon might seem like a bit much. But then isn't that
what a weekend nap is for?

Christie Ever attuned to my French heritage, I insist that any egg
dish be accompanied by a simple green salad. When we're ready to
eat, we check our wine stash for a crisp, refreshing light white, like a
Petit Chablis or Muscadet, to pour for our brunch—also very French.

QUICK IDEAS *for* SMOOTHIES

Smoothies are one of our favorite weekday breakfasts. They're an efficient way to consume a concentrated dose of fruit nutrition, easy to vary by season and preference, and take only minutes to make. Plus, they're delicious and refreshing.

Our freezer is loaded with nearly every kind of frozen fruit imaginable. We like to use frozen over fresh because we never have to add ice cubes to our smoothies, which can dilute them. We also keep a variety of juices around to vary the flavor. Apple cider is a favorite, as are the more exotic pineapple, guava, and mango. Greek-style yogurt is another common addition, delivering a creamy texture and plenty of protein and vitamins.

STRAWBERRY-BANANA

Blend 1 frozen banana + handful frozen strawberries + splash apple cider + heaping spoonful plain yogurt.

BANANA-CINNAMON

Blend 2 frozen bananas + splash fresh orange juice + heaping spoonful plain yogurt + splash half-and-half + 2 pinches ground cinnamon.

TROPICAL BERRY

Blend 1 frozen banana + handful each frozen blueberries and blackberries + splash guava nectar + splash unsweetened coconut milk.

PEACH POWER

Blend 2 handfuls frozen peaches + ½ frozen banana + splash peach nectar + heaping spoonful plain yogurt + pinch white pepper + pinch ground cardamom.

QUICK IDEAS *for* EGG SCRAMBLES

Egg scrambles are one of our go-to weekend meals and are great "kitchen sink" dishes. In other words, you really don't need a recipe and you can use whatever bits of cheese, meat, vegetables, and fresh herbs you have on hand.

To make scrambles, first cook any raw meats, or sauté or steam any raw vegetables until soft and tender. Transfer to a plate. Crack the eggs into a bowl, add a pinch each of salt and pepper, and whisk just until blended. Add a dab of butter to a frying pan and warm over medium heat. When the butter foams, add the eggs and cook, stirring, just until curds form, 1½–2 minutes. Add the cooked meat or vegetables, cheese, toasted bread, and/or herbs and continue to cook, stirring, for 2–3 minutes longer. Spoon onto plates and serve with hot-pepper sauce and toast. Each recipe serves 2.

BACON-PARMESAN
1 Tbsp butter + 4 large eggs + handful toasted French bread cubes + 4 slices bacon, cooked and crumbled + grated Parmesan cheese + chopped fresh flat-leaf parsley.

BROCCOLI-POTATO
1 Tbsp butter + 4 large eggs + 2 handfuls steamed broccoli + 1 handful diced cooked potatoes + shredded Gruyère cheese + pinch dried dill.

SPINACH-CHEDDAR
1 Tbsp butter + 4 large eggs + 2 handfuls baby spinach, wilted + shredded white Cheddar cheese.

RICOTTA-CHIVE
1 Tbsp butter + 4 large eggs + 1 bunch fresh chives, chopped + heaping spoonful ricotta cheese.

DENVER
1 Tbsp butter + 4 large eggs + handful chopped mushrooms, sautéed + ½ yellow onion, diced and sautéed + diced cooked ham.

TOMATO-MINT
1 Tbsp butter + 4 large eggs + 1 shallot, chopped and sautéed + 1 tomato, chopped + chopped fresh mint.

GRANOLA WITH GREEK YOGURT AND HONEY

We discovered the inspired combination of yogurt and honey in Greece. A drizzle of intensely flavored honey delivers a delicious counterpoint to the bright tang of Greek-style yogurt, which is creamier and tastier than most commercially available yogurt. Pair this combo with crunchy homemade granola and fresh fruit for an easy and well-rounded breakfast.

INGREDIENTS

FOR THE GRANOLA

3 cups (9 oz/280 g) old-fashioned rolled oats

¼ cup (1 oz/30 g) walnuts, coarsely chopped

¼ cup (1 oz/30 g) almonds, coarsely chopped

¼ cup (1½ oz/45 g) cashew halves

2 Tbsp unsweetened shredded dried coconut

¼ cup (2½ oz/75 g) maple syrup

1 tsp vanilla extract

¼ cup (2 fl oz/60 ml) sesame oil

½ cup (3 oz/90 g) dried apricots, cut into pieces

½ cup (3 oz/90 g) dried cranberries

2 cups (16 oz/500 g) Greek-style plain yogurt

2 cups (8 oz/250 g) mixed berries (optional)

¼ cup (3 oz/90 g) honey

TOOLS

chef's knife, assorted mixing bowls, rimmed baking sheet

Preheat the oven to 325°F (165°C).

To make the granola, in a large bowl, stir together the oats, walnuts, almonds, cashews, and coconut. In a small bowl, stir together the maple syrup, vanilla, and sesame oil. Drizzle the maple syrup mixture over the oat mixture and stir to moisten evenly. Spread the oat mixture on a rimmed baking sheet in an even layer.

Bake, stirring about every 7 minutes, until the oats just begin to turn golden, about 30 minutes total. The granola should feel dry rather than moist, but it will not turn crisp until it cools. When the oats are golden, remove from the oven and stir in the apricots and cranberries. Let cool on the baking sheet. Store in an airtight container at room temperature for up to 1 week.

Serve the granola with the yogurt and berries, if using, and pass the honey for drizzling over the top.

SERVES 4

OLD-FASHIONED OATMEAL
WITH RASPBERRY COMPOTE

Nothing is more warming on a cold morning than a bowl of steaming oatmeal. Here, it is topped with raspberries in an almond-scented syrup. Cooking the oats in milk, even nonfat milk, rather than water gives them a rich, creamy consistency. Be sure to use old-fashioned rolled oats, not quick-cooking oats, for their nutty flavor and superior texture.

INGREDIENTS

FOR THE RASPBERRY COMPOTE

½ cup (4 oz/125 g) sugar

2 tsp fresh lemon juice

¼ tsp almond extract

1 cup (4 oz/125 g) raspberries

FOR THE OATMEAL

4 cups (32 fl oz/1 l) whole milk

¼ tsp salt

2 cups (6 oz/185 g) old-fashioned rolled oats

TOOLS

chef's knife, citrus reamer or press, small saucepan, heatproof mixing bowl, saucepan

To make the raspberry compote, in a small saucepan over low heat, combine ½ cup (4 fl oz/125 ml) water and the sugar and cook, stirring, until the sugar dissolves. Remove from the heat and pour the sugar syrup into a heatproof bowl. Stir in the lemon juice and almond extract. Let the syrup cool to room temperature, then gently stir in the raspberries. Set aside.

To make the oatmeal, in a saucepan over medium-high heat, bring the milk and salt to a gentle boil, about 3 minutes. Slowly stir in the oats. Reduce the heat to medium and cook uncovered at a gentle boil, stirring frequently and adjusting the heat as needed, until the oatmeal is soft and the milk is absorbed, about 10 minutes. Remove from the heat, cover, and let stand for 3 minutes.

Spoon the hot oatmeal into individual bowls, divide the compote among the bowls, and serve.

SERVES 4

BROILED GRAPEFRUIT WITH BROWN SUGAR

You can use any variety of grapefruit here. White grapefruits are more tart than the pink and ruby types, however, so they will benefit more from the addition of the brown-sugar topping.

INGREDIENTS

3 grapefruits, halved

6 Tbsp (3 oz/90 g) firmly packed light brown sugar

TOOLS

chef's knife, rimmed baking sheet

Preheat the broiler. Line a rimmed baking sheet with foil.

Arrange the grapefruit halves, cut sides up, on the prepared baking sheet. Sprinkle each half with 1 tablespoon of the brown sugar. Broil until the sugar has melted and is bubbling, 2–3 minutes. Transfer to a platter or individual bowls and serve.

SERVES 6

CRANBERRY-ORANGE MUFFINS

When fresh cranberries appear in fall and winter, buy a few extra bags and freeze them for use in muffins and quick breads year-round.

INGREDIENTS

4 Tbsp (2 oz/60 g) butter, melted, plus more for muffin pan

2 cups (10 oz/315 g) all-purpose flour

½ cup (4 oz/125 g) granulated sugar

½ cup (3½ oz/105 g) firmly packed light brown sugar

2 tsp baking powder

½ tsp salt

Grated zest of 1 orange

1 large egg

½ cup (4 fl oz/125 ml) whole milk

½ cup (4 fl oz/125 ml) fresh orange juice

1½ cups (6 oz/185 g) fresh or unthawed frozen cranberries

½ cup (2 oz/60 g) walnuts, chopped

TOOLS

rasp grater, chef's knife, citrus reamer or press, 12-cup muffin pan, 2 mixing bowls, whisk, silicone spatula, wire rack

Preheat the oven to 350°F (180°C). Butter 10 standard muffin cups.

In a bowl, stir together the flour, sugars, baking powder, salt, and zest. In another bowl, whisk together the egg, melted butter, milk, and orange juice until blended. Add to the dry ingredients, stirring until evenly moistened. Using a silicone spatula, fold in the cranberries and nuts just until evenly distributed. Spoon into the prepared muffin cups, dividing the batter evenly.

Bake until the muffins are golden and a toothpick inserted into the center comes out clean, 20–25 minutes. Let cool in the pan on a wire rack for 5 minutes, then unmold and serve.

MAKES 10 MUFFINS

SCONES WITH RAISINS AND LEMON ZEST

These crumbly scones are easier to make than they look, which means you can get them into the oven and still have plenty of time to enjoy your morning. For the best results, mix the dough with a light touch and bake it as soon as it is shaped. Serve fresh out of the oven, with butter and berry preserves.

INGREDIENTS

FOR THE DOUGH

2 cups (10 oz/315 g) all-purpose flour

¼ cup (2 oz/60 g) granulated sugar

1 Tbsp baking powder

½ tsp salt

2 tsp grated lemon zest

6 Tbsp (3 oz/90 g) cold butter, cut into ½-inch (12-mm) pieces

½ cup (3 oz/90 g) raisins or dried currants

¾ cup (6 fl oz/180 ml) heavy cream

FOR THE TOPPING

1 Tbsp granulated, Demerara, or turbinado sugar

1 tsp ground cinnamon

2 tsp whole milk or heavy cream

TOOLS

rasp grater, chef's knife, rimless baking sheet, assorted mixing bowls, pastry blender (optional) and silicone spatula or food processor, 3-inch (7.5-cm) biscuit cutter (optional), pastry brush, wire rack

Preheat the oven to 425°F (220°C). Line a rimless baking sheet with parchment paper.

To mix by hand, in a bowl, stir together the flour, ¼ cup sugar, baking powder, salt, and lemon zest. Using a pastry blender or 2 knives, cut in the butter until it is broken down into unevenly sized pieces, the largest as big as a pea. Stir in the raisins. Pour the cream over the dry ingredients and mix with a silicone spatula just until the dry ingredients are moistened.

To mix by food processor, combine the flour, ¼ cup sugar, baking powder, salt, and lemon zest in a food processor and pulse 2 or 3 times to mix. Add the butter and pulse 7 or 8 times, just until it is broken down into unevenly sized pieces, the largest as big as a pea. Pour in the cream and pulse just until moistened. Scatter the raisins over the dough.

Turn the dough out onto a lightly floured work surface and press gently until the dough clings together in a ball. Pat out into a round about ½ inch (12 mm) thick and 6½ inches (16.5 cm) in diameter. Cut the round into 6 wedges, or use a 3-inch (7.5-cm) biscuit cutter to cut out rounds. Place 1 inch (2.5 cm) apart on the prepared baking sheet.

To make the topping, in a small bowl, stir together the 1 tablespoon sugar and cinnamon. Brush the tops of the scones with the milk and sprinkle evenly with the cinnamon sugar.

Bake the scones until they are golden brown, 13–17 minutes. Transfer to a wire rack. Serve hot, warm, or at room temperature. Store in an airtight container at room temperature for up to 2 days.

MAKES 6 SCONES

BLUEBERRY PANCAKES

To give your spouse a treat, halve the recipe and serve the pancakes as breakfast in bed. For a nice touch, heat a pitcher of maple syrup by warming it in a saucepan of water over low heat or by putting it in the microwave for several seconds.

INGREDIENTS

1½ cups (7½ oz/235 g) all-purpose flour

2 Tbsp sugar

1½ tsp baking powder

1 tsp baking soda

¾ tsp salt

2 large eggs, separated

2 cups (16 fl oz/500 ml) buttermilk

4 Tbsp (2 oz/60 g) butter, melted, plus more melted butter for brushing

1½ cups (6 oz/185 g) blueberries

Maple syrup, warmed, for serving

TOOLS

assorted mixing bowls, whisk, electric mixer, silicone spatula, griddle or large frying pan, pastry brush, ladle, metal spatula, baking sheet

Preheat the oven to 200°F (95°C).

In a large bowl, whisk together the flour, sugar, baking powder, baking soda, and salt. In another bowl, whisk together the egg yolks, buttermilk, and the 4 tablespoons butter. Add the egg yolk mixture to the flour mixture and stir just until blended.

In another large bowl, using an electric mixer on high speed, beat the egg whites until soft peaks form. Gently fold the whites into the batter with a silicone spatula just until no white streaks remain.

Heat a griddle or large frying pan, preferably nonstick, over medium heat until a drop of water flicked on the surface sizzles and then immediately evaporates. Brush lightly with butter. For each pancake, ladle ⅓ cup (3 fl oz/ 80 ml) batter onto the griddle and use the back of the ladle to spread gently into a 4-inch (10-cm) circle. Sprinkle evenly with about 2 tablespoons blueberries. Cook until large bubbles form on the top and pop and the edges of the pancakes are lightly browned, about 2 minutes. Flip the pancakes and cook the other side until lightly browned, 1½–2 minutes longer. Transfer to a baking sheet and place in the oven to keep warm; do not cover the pancakes, or they will get soggy. Repeat with the remaining batter, brushing the pan with more butter as needed.

When all of the pancakes are cooked, serve warm with the maple syrup.

MAKES ABOUT 12 PANCAKES; SERVES 4

LEMON-RICOTTA PANCAKES

Ricotta and beaten egg whites give these pancakes a light, fluffy texture. When you ladle the batter into the pan, make sure the butter is bubbling but not browned, or its flavor will taint the pancakes. Pass additional butter at the table for anyone who desires a little extra richness.

INGREDIENTS

1½ cups (7½ oz/235 g) all-purpose flour

1 tsp baking soda

½ tsp salt

1½ cups (12 fl oz/375 ml) buttermilk

2 large eggs, separated

¼ cup (2 oz/60 g) sugar

¾ cup (6 oz/185 g) whole-milk or part-skim ricotta cheese

1 Tbsp grated lemon zest

Butter, melted, for brushing

12 strawberries, hulled, sliced, and tossed with 1 Tbsp sugar

TOOLS

rasp grater, paring knife, assorted mixing bowls, whisk, electric mixer, silicone spatula, griddle or large frying pan, pastry brush, ladle, metal spatula, baking sheet

Preheat the oven to 200°F (95°C).

In a large bowl, whisk together the flour, baking soda, and salt. In another bowl, whisk together the buttermilk, egg yolks, sugar, cheese, and lemon zest. Add the buttermilk mixture to the flour mixture and stir just until blended. Some small lumps will remain.

In another large bowl, using an electric mixer on high speed, beat the egg whites until soft peaks form. Gently fold the whites into the ricotta mixture with a silicone spatula just until no white streaks remain.

Heat a griddle or large frying pan, preferably nonstick, over medium heat until a drop of water flicked onto the surface sizzles and then immediately evaporates. Brush with melted butter. For each pancake, ladle about ¼ cup (2 fl oz/60 ml) batter onto the griddle. Reduce the heat to medium-low and cook until small bubbles appear on the top, the edges start to look dry, and the bottoms are golden brown, about 4 minutes. Using a metal spatula, carefully flip the pancakes and cook the other side until lightly browned, about 1½ minutes longer. Transfer to a baking sheet and place in the oven to keep warm; do not cover the pancakes, or they will get soggy. Repeat with the remaining batter, brushing the pan with more butter as needed.

When all of the pancakes are cooked, serve warm, accompanied with the strawberries.

MAKES ABOUT 12 PANCAKES; SERVES 4

RAISED WAFFLES WITH STRAWBERRY-RHUBARB COMPOTE

The batter for these extra-crisp, yeast-leavened waffles is quickly mixed the night before serving, so it is ready to pour into the waffle iron first thing in the morning. The compote can be made up to 2 days in advance and refrigerated.

INGREDIENTS

FOR THE STRAWBERRY-RHUBARB COMPOTE

4 cups (1½ lb/750 g) coarsely chopped rhubarb stalks

¼ cup (2 oz/60 g) granulated sugar

1½ cups (6 oz/185 g) strawberries, hulled and halved

FOR THE WAFFLES

1 package (2½ tsp) active dry yeast

1 tsp granulated sugar

¼ cup (2 fl oz/60 ml) warm water (105°–115°F/ 40°–46°C)

1 cup (8 fl oz/250 ml) whole milk

2 Tbsp butter

1 cup (5 oz/155 g) all-purpose flour

2 Tbsp firmly packed light brown sugar

¼ tsp salt

Canola oil for brushing

1 large egg, lightly beaten

¼ tsp baking soda

TOOLS

chef's knife, paring knife, instant-read thermometer (optional), 2 saucepans, assorted mixing bowls, whisk, waffle iron, pastry brush, ladle, small spatula, baking sheet

To make the strawberry-rhubarb compote, in a saucepan over medium heat, combine the rhubarb, ¼ cup granulated sugar, and ¼ cup (2 fl oz/60 ml) water. Cook until the mixture comes to a simmer and the rhubarb begins to release its liquid, about 10 minutes, then stir in the strawberries. Simmer gently until the rhubarb is soft when pierced with a fork, about 10 minutes. Skim any foam from the top. Let cool, cover, and refrigerate until serving.

To make the waffles, in a large bowl, dissolve the yeast and 1 teaspoon sugar in the warm water and let stand until foamy, about 5 minutes. In a saucepan over low heat, combine the milk and butter and heat to warm (about 115°F/46°C).

In a small bowl, whisk together the flour, brown sugar, and salt. Stir the warm milk mixture into the bowl with the dissolved yeast. Add the flour mixture and stir until blended. Cover the bowl and refrigerate overnight. The batter will thicken slightly.

To cook the waffles, preheat the oven to 200°F (95°C). Preheat a waffle iron for 5 minutes, then brush with oil. Add the egg and baking soda to the chilled batter and stir until blended. Ladle enough batter for 1 waffle into the center of the waffle iron (usually about ½ cup/4 fl oz/125 ml), and spread with a small spatula. Close the waffle iron and cook until the waffle is browned and crisp, according to the manufacturer's directions (usually 4–5 minutes). Transfer the waffle to a baking sheet and keep warm in the oven. Repeat with the remaining batter. Meanwhile, warm the compote over low heat.

Serve the waffles warm, accompanied with the warmed compote.

SERVES 4

in the kitchen with

JULIE *and* MATT WALKER

Our favorite comfort food

Tunis-Letta. This is the made-up name for a sandwich we ate often in the first year of marriage. We mix albacore tuna with olive oil, mayo, relish, and peppers or pepperoncini and wrap it in lettuce. It's simple but tasty.

Cooking style

We generally go for easy recipes with fresh ingredients. Someone once told us that meals don't have to be difficult to be good, you just have to use quality ingredients. We try to follow that creed.

Kitchen strength as a couple

We are always up for a challenge and not intimidated by a recipe. There are some nights that we spend thrashing our kitchen and using every mixing bowl and measuring spoon we own. We enjoy the adventure of cooking together.

Maintaining kitchen bliss

Work as a team. Split up the meal and work together to get it done. During clean up, we like to talk about the tasty food we just ate. A favorite question is: "What would you think if served this dish at a restaurant?"

Lazy morning breakfast

We love omelets stuffed with anything fresh. If we have some potatoes, we'll go for homemade hash browns, too.

Favorite home-cooked meal for two

We love homemade pizza with healthy toppings like heirloom tomatoes and basil combined with thin slices of mozzarella and prosciutto.

BAKED FRENCH TOAST

This delicious spiced toast is quickly assembled and can then be left to bake while you ready other parts of the meal. For a hint of orange, add a splash of Grand Marnier to the melted butter before you brush it on the toast.

INGREDIENTS

1 cup (8 fl oz/250 ml) half-and-half or whole milk

4 large eggs

2 Tbsp firmly packed light brown sugar

½ tsp ground cinnamon

¼ tsp freshly grated nutmeg

¼ tsp salt

12 slices sweet French bread or other bread

2 Tbsp butter, melted

Maple syrup, warmed, for serving

TOOLS

nutmeg grater or rasp grater, serrated bread knife, rimmed baking sheets, mixing bowl, whisk, pastry brush

Preheat the oven to 400°F (200°C). Line rimmed baking sheets with parchment paper or foil.

In a shallow bowl, whisk together the half-and-half, eggs, brown sugar, cinnamon, nutmeg, and salt. One slice at a time, turn the bread in the egg mixture to coat on both sides, soaking each slice for about 30 seconds. Shake off the excess batter and transfer the soaked bread to the prepared baking sheet.

Bake until the tops are golden, 5–7 minutes. Flip each slice and continue to bake until puffed and golden on the second side, 5–7 minutes longer.

Turn the oven to the broiler setting. Brush the tops of the baked toasts with the melted butter. Place under the broiler until lightly browned, about 1 minute. Serve warm, with the maple syrup.

SERVES 6

CINNAMON-WALNUT COFFEE CAKE

The cinnamon-walnut mixture is used twice here: it is swirled through the center of the fine-crumbed cake, and it forms the crunchy topping. You can bake the cake up to 3 days in advance, cover it with plastic wrap, and store it at room temperature, making it a great addition to a big brunch menu.

INGREDIENTS

FOR THE FILLING AND TOPPING

1 cup (4 oz/125 g) finely chopped walnuts

⅓ cup (3 oz/90 g) granulated sugar

2 tsp ground cinnamon

2¾ cups (11 oz/345 g) cake flour

1 tsp baking powder

½ tsp baking soda

½ tsp salt

3 large eggs

2 cups (1 lb/500 g) granulated sugar

1 cup (8 fl oz/250 ml) canola or corn oil

2 tsp vanilla extract

1 cup (8 oz/250 g) sour cream

Confectioners' sugar for dusting

TOOLS

chef's knife, 10-inch (25-cm) tube pan, assorted mixing bowls, sifter, electric mixer, silicone spatula, small knife, toothpick, wire rack, fine-mesh sieve

Preheat the oven to 350°F (180°C). Oil a 10-inch (25-cm) tube pan with sides at least 3¾ inches (9.5 cm) high. Line the bottom with parchment paper and oil the paper.

To make the filling and topping, in a bowl, stir together the walnuts, sugar, and cinnamon. Set aside.

In a large bowl, sift together the flour, baking powder, baking soda, and salt.

In another large bowl, using an electric mixer on medium speed, beat together the eggs and granulated sugar until the mixture is light in color and fluffy, about 2 minutes. On low speed, slowly add the oil and vanilla and beat until well mixed. Add the dry ingredients and beat just until incorporated. Mix in the sour cream until no white streaks remain.

Pour about two-thirds of the batter into the prepared pan and smooth the top with a silicone spatula. Set aside ¼ cup (2 oz/60 g) of the walnut-cinnamon mixture to use as a topping. Sprinkle the remaining mixture evenly over the batter. Insert a small knife about halfway into the batter and gently swirl the walnut-cinnamon mixture through the batter. Pour the remaining batter evenly over the filling and smooth the top with the spatula. Sprinkle evenly with the reserved topping.

Bake until a toothpick inserted near the center of the cake comes out clean, about 55 minutes. Transfer to a wire rack and let cool for 15 minutes. Run the small knife around the sides and center tube of the pan to loosen. Invert the wire rack on top of the pan and invert both the rack and the pan. Lift off the pan and remove and discard the parchment. Turn the cake topping side up and let cool completely on the rack. Just before serving, use a fine-mesh sieve to dust the cake with confectioners' sugar.

SERVES 12

TOMATO AND FETA TART

You don't need to be an expert baker to make this tart. Store-bought puff pastry dough is treated to a simple topping of tomatoes, cheese, and herbs, and then baked until the dough is golden brown and flaky. You can make the tart year-round, trading out the tomatoes for other seasonal vegetables and using your favorite cheeses in place of the feta.

INGREDIENTS

1 sheet frozen puff pastry, about 9 oz (280 g), thawed according to package directions

1 cup (6 oz/185 g) ripe cherry tomatoes, halved

8 ripe tomatoes, thinly sliced

6 oz (185 g) feta cheese, crumbled

1 Tbsp chopped fresh oregano

Salt and freshly ground pepper

6 sprigs fresh thyme

TOOLS

rimmed baking sheet, chef's knife, rolling pin

DRINK NOTE

Pour a sparkling wine with this casual tart for brunch. Or, reach for a racy Sauvignon Blanc from New Zealand, Chile, or France. Or, for a wonderful unusual option, try a Greek white wine—bright, punchy Assyrtiko from the island of Santorini is a good match with the tangy cheese and tomatoes.

Preheat the oven to 400°F (200°C). Line a rimmed baking sheet with parchment paper.

Unfold the pastry sheet on a lightly floured work surface. Roll out into a 9-by-13-inch (23-by-33-cm) rectangle about ⅛ inch (3 mm) thick. Transfer the rectangle to the prepared baking sheet. Using a fork, prick the rectangle evenly all over. To create a border on the tart, fold over ½ inch (12 mm) of the pastry all the way around the edge.

Arrange the cherry tomato halves, sliced tomatoes, and cheese evenly on top of the pastry rectangle. Sprinkle evenly with the oregano, season with salt and pepper, and top with the thyme sprigs.

Bake until the pastry is puffed and golden brown, about 20 minutes. Remove from the oven and transfer to a work surface. Cut the tart into pieces and serve.

SERVES 4–6

CLASSIC OMELET WITH
MASCARPONE AND HERBS

This authentic French rolled omelet—tender and plump on the outside and creamy on the inside—also makes a great centerpiece for a midweek supper, accompanied with a green salad and a good white wine. Because you can cook only one omelet at a time, serve each one as it is ready, or keep the first one loosely tented with foil while you prepare the second.

INGREDIENTS

3 large eggs

Salt

2 Tbsp mascarpone cheese

2 tsp finely chopped fresh chives

2 tsp finely chopped fresh chervil

1 tsp finely chopped fresh flat-leaf parsley

1 Tbsp butter

TOOLS

chef's knife, small mixing bowl, 7- or 8-inch (18- or 20-cm) nonstick frying pan or omelet pan, silicone spatula

In a small bowl, beat the eggs lightly with a fork to blend the yolks and whites completely. Add 1 tablespoon water, a pinch of salt, the cheese, and the chives, chervil, and parsley and beat briefly to mix. Do not overbeat.

In a 7- or 8-inch (18- or 20-cm) nonstick frying pan or omelet pan over medium-high heat, melt the butter. When the butter stops foaming but before it begins to brown, add the egg mixture to the pan. When the eggs begin to set on the bottom, after about 30 seconds, use a small silicone spatula to pull in the egg mixture from the sides of the pan toward the center to allow the raw egg to run underneath the cooked egg. Repeat 2 or 3 times, until most of the bottom is set but the surface remains moist and creamy.

Tilt the pan toward you, sliding the omelet up the side of the pan. Use the spatula to fold in the edge of the omelet, then roll it up. Flip the omelet once or twice with the spatula to secure the roll. Slide the omelet onto a plate and serve.

SERVES 1

SCRAMBLED EGGS WITH
MUSHROOMS, CHEDDAR, AND PANCETTA

Here, the winning combination of wild mushrooms, cheese, and pancetta transforms everyday scrambled eggs into something special. We often use a different herb, such as thyme or basil, for the parsley, and Gruyère or mozzarella for the Cheddar. You can substitute cultivated mushrooms for some or all of the wild ones.

INGREDIENTS

4 Tbsp (2 oz/60 g) butter

½ lb (250 g) wild mushrooms such as chanterelle, porcini, or black trumpet, coarsely chopped

Salt and freshly ground pepper

10 large eggs

1 clove garlic, minced

2 oz (60 g) thinly sliced pancetta, cut into ½-inch (12-mm) pieces

¼ lb (125 g) Cheddar cheese, cut into ½-inch (12-mm) cubes

2 Tbsp minced fresh flat-leaf parsley

TOOLS

chef's knife, frying pan, slotted spoon, assorted mixing bowls, whisk

DRINK NOTE

For brunch, eggs and mushrooms are friendly with earthy whites and reds. Look for a Chenin Blanc from the Loire Valley or a Chardonnay from Burgundy or the West Coast of the U.S. (make sure it's not too oaky). For a red, try a Côtes du Rhône or Pinot Noir.

In a frying pan over medium-high heat, melt 1½ tablespoons of the butter. When it foams, add the mushrooms and sauté until they release their juices, 4–5 minutes. Sprinkle with ¼ teaspoon salt. Using a slotted spoon, transfer to a bowl and set aside. Rinse out the frying pan.

Break the eggs into a separate bowl, add ¾ teaspoon salt and ½ teaspoon pepper, and whisk until well blended.

Return the frying pan to medium heat and melt the remaining 2½ tablespoons butter. When it foams, add the garlic and pancetta and sauté until translucent, 2–3 minutes. Pour in the eggs and reduce the heat to low. Cook, stirring often, until the eggs are nearly cooked to the desired consistency, about 5 minutes for soft eggs and 7–8 minutes for firmer ones. Add the mushrooms, cheese, and parsley during the last 2 minutes of cooking, stirring gently. Spoon the eggs onto plates and serve.

SERVES 6

EGGS BENEDICT

Serve eggs Benedict for a Mother's Day brunch or an Easter celebration, or treat your houseguests—or just yourselves—on a Sunday morning. Adding spinach turns the dish into eggs Florentine. In spring, use sliced steamed asparagus in place of the spinach.

INGREDIENTS

FOR THE HOLLANDAISE SAUCE

4 large egg yolks, at room temperature

1 Tbsp fresh lemon juice

Salt

¼ tsp cayenne pepper

1 cup (8 oz/250 g) butter

2 tsp extra-virgin olive oil (optional)

1½ lb (750 g) baby spinach (optional)

Salt and freshly ground black pepper

8 large eggs

4 English muffins, split and toasted

8 slices country ham or prosciutto, at room temperature

TOOLS

chef's knife, citrus reamer or press, toaster or toaster oven, blender, small saucepan, whisk, 1 or 2 large sauté pans, 4 small ramekins, slotted spoon, paring knife

To make the hollandaise sauce, in a blender, combine the egg yolks, 1 tablespoon water, the lemon juice, ¼ teaspoon salt, and the cayenne. In a small saucepan over medium heat, melt the butter. With the blender running, slowly add the warm melted butter through the vent in the lid, processing until the sauce is thick and smooth. Taste and adjust the seasoning. If the sauce is too thick, add a bit more water to thin it. Transfer to a bowl, cover, and set aside.

If using the spinach, in a large sauté pan over medium-low heat, warm the oil. Add the spinach and sauté gently just until tender, about 4 minutes. Season with ½ teaspoon salt, remove from the heat, and keep warm.

Meanwhile, poach the eggs: Pour water to a depth of 3 inches (7.5 cm) into a large sauté pan, add a pinch of salt, and bring to a simmer over medium heat. Working with 4 eggs at a time, crack each egg into a small ramekin and carefully slip the egg into the water. Adjust the heat so that the water barely simmers. Poach the eggs for 3–5 minutes, then remove from the water with a slotted spoon and place on a paper towel–lined plate. Repeat to poach the remaining 4 eggs. Using a paring knife, trim any straggly edges from the egg whites.

Place 2 English muffin halves, cut side up, on each of 4 plates. Lay a ham slice on each muffin half. Arrange the warm spinach, if using, on the ham, top with a poached egg, and spoon ¼ cup (2 fl oz/60 ml) warm hollandaise sauce over each egg. Grind pepper over the top and serve.

SERVES 4

MUSHROOM, GOAT CHEESE, AND HERB FRITTATA

This hearty, rustic dish is a welcome addition to nearly any morning get-together. We also like the fact that it can be made in advance and served at room temperature, which allows us to be more relaxed around our guests. For the best flavor, pick up the eggs for this dish at your local farmers' market.

INGREDIENTS

4 Tbsp (2 fl oz/60 ml) extra-virgin olive oil

2 shallots, finely chopped

1 cup (3 oz/90 g) chopped mixed mushrooms

1 tsp minced fresh thyme, or ½ tsp dried thyme

1 tsp minced fresh oregano, or ½ tsp dried oregano

¼ tsp red pepper flakes

Salt and freshly ground pepper

10 large eggs

3 Tbsp heavy cream

¼ lb (125 g) fresh goat cheese, crumbled

⅓ cup (1½ oz/45 g) freshly grated Parmesan cheese

TOOLS

chef's knife, rasp grater, large oven-safe frying pan, mixing bowl, spatula

Preheat the broiler.

In a large oven-safe frying pan over medium-high heat, warm 1 tablespoon of the olive oil. Add the shallots, mushrooms, thyme, oregano, and red pepper flakes, season with salt and pepper, and sauté, stirring often, until the shallots are soft and the mushrooms have released most of their liquid, 5–7 minutes. Remove from the heat.

In a bowl, using a fork, beat together the eggs, cream, ½ teaspoon salt, and 4 or 5 grinds of pepper until blended. Add the shallot-mushroom mixture and the goat cheese and set aside.

Rinse out the frying pan, place it over medium-high heat, and warm the remaining 3 tablespoons oil. Pour in the egg mixture, spreading the vegetables in an even layer. As the eggs set around the edges of the pan, lift the edges of the frittata with a spatula and tilt the pan to allow the liquid egg in the center to run underneath. Cook until the eggs are firmly set along the edges but the center is still runny, 10–15 minutes.

Sprinkle the Parmesan over the frittata and place under the broiler until the top is set and golden, about 2 minutes. Carefully remove the pan from the broiler. Loosen the edges of the frittata and slide it onto a serving plate. Let cool for 15 minutes. Cut into wedges and serve warm or at room temperature.

SERVES 4–6

HUEVOS RANCHEROS

If you're pressed for time (or just feeling lazy), you can use store-bought salsa for this dish. That said, the fresh salsa is quick and easy to make and is worth the extra effort. If you cannot fry all of the eggs at once, hold the finished plates in a warm spot until all of the eggs are cooked and plated.

INGREDIENTS

FOR THE SALSA

2 Tbsp finely chopped yellow onion

2 small to medium ripe tomatoes, cored and chopped

2 Tbsp chopped fresh cilantro

Salt

2 tsp fresh lime juice, or as needed

1 Tbsp minced jalapeño chile

1 Tbsp red wine vinegar

1 can (14 oz/440 g) regular or spicy refried beans

8 corn tortillas, 6 inches (15 cm) in diameter

Extra-virgin olive oil for frying

8 large eggs

1 avocado, pitted, peeled, and sliced

TOOLS

chef's knife, citrus reamer or press, mixing bowl, small saucepan, large frying pan, spatula

To make the salsa, in a bowl, combine the onion, tomatoes, cilantro, ½ teaspoon salt, the lime juice, jalapeño, and vinegar and stir to blend. Add 1 tablespoon water if the mixture seems dry. Taste the salsa and adjust the seasoning with salt and lime juice if needed. Let stand for 10 minutes to allow the flavors to marry.

In a small saucepan over medium-high heat, combine the beans and ¼ cup (2 fl oz/60 ml) water and cook, stirring often, until hot, about 7 minutes. Set aside and cover to keep warm.

Heat a large frying pan over high heat and add the tortillas, one at a time, heating each for a minute or two on each side. Wrap in a clean kitchen towel to keep warm.

To fry the eggs, return the frying pan to medium-high heat and coat with a thin film of oil. Working in batches, break the eggs into the pan, spacing them about 1 inch (2.5 cm) apart. Reduce the heat to low, cover the pan, and cook until the whites are set and the yolks are nearly set, 5–7 minutes.

Just before the eggs are ready, place 2 tortillas on each of 4 plates and spread each tortilla with an equal quantity of the beans. Using a metal spatula, top each tortilla with an egg. Top the eggs with a little salsa and with the avocado slices and serve. Pass the remaining salsa at the table.

SERVES 4

BAKED EGGS WITH HAM, BRIE, AND CHIVES

For a vegetarian version of this dish, substitute 1 cup (3 oz/90 g) sliced mushrooms, sautéed until tender, for the ham. Other soft cheeses, such as Camembert, Taleggio, or a creamy fresh goat cheese, will work in place of the Brie. For added ease, assemble the ramekins the night before, cover with plastic wrap, and refrigerate until ready to bake.

INGREDIENTS

4 Tbsp (2 oz/60 g) butter

8 large eggs

2 slices ham, cut into narrow strips

¼ lb (125 g) Brie cheese, end rind removed, cut into small cubes

2 Tbsp chopped fresh chives

Salt and freshly ground pepper

8 slices brioche or sourdough bread, toasted

TOOLS

chef's knife, toaster or toaster oven, teakettle, four ¾-cup (6–fl oz/180-ml) ramekins, small baking pan

DRINK NOTE

Pairing young, fresh reds with eggs and ham is a specialty of Burgundy, one of our favorite wine regions. In that spirit, try a vibrant Pinot Noir from Burgundy, Oregon, or California. A French Beaujolais, served on the cool side, also works well.

Preheat the oven to 375°F (190°C). Bring a teakettle filled with water to a boil. Place four ¾-cup (6–fl oz/180-ml) ramekins in a small baking pan.

Place 1 tablespoon of the butter in each ramekin, and then carefully break 2 eggs into each ramekin. Scatter the ham strips and Brie cubes evenly over the eggs. Sprinkle with the chives and season with salt and pepper.

Carefully pour the boiling water into the baking pan to reach halfway up the sides of the ramekins. Cover the pan with foil and bake until the egg whites are firm but the yolks are still soft, 10–12 minutes.

Remove the pan from the oven and carefully remove the ramekins from the water bath. Set each ramekin on an individual plate, place 2 toast slices on the side of each plate, and serve.

SERVES 4

in the kitchen with

SAUKOK *and* JAMIE TIAMPO

Favorite everyday ingredient
Lemons—a little splash of freshly squeezed lemon juice perks up nearly any dish, and lemon zest adds a touch of freshness.

Lazy morning breakfast
Scrambled eggs with caramelized onions and goat cheese.

Secret culinary weapon
Jamie's preserved Meyer lemons. They are simple to make, yet add a complex flavor and umami to any dish.

Grandest food-love gesture
While Jamie and I were dating long distance, he learned that I adore spaghetti with meat sauce. After visiting him in San Francisco one weekend, I flew back to New York and was surprised to find a FedEx package filled with an ice-packed container of homemade Bolognese at my door.

Always in the fridge
Butter, lemons, soy sauce, Sriracha, black bean sauce, kim chee, Dijon mustard, tahini, Thai chiles, Parmigiano-Reggiano, and good white wine.

Favorite home-cooked meal for two
We make a pot of meat sauce over the weekend, and then use it for meals the following week. We never get tired of a bowl of pasta and a salad.

Kitchen secret
Clean as you go and prep ahead of time. Keep ingredients in separate prep bowls so everything will be ready and within reach while cooking.

FRIED EGGS WITH ASPARAGUS, PANCETTA, AND BREAD CRUMBS

Resting a fried egg with a still-runny yolk on top of any roasted or sautéed vegetable is a perfect recipe, as the soft, thick yolk flows easily over the vegetable, becoming a simple, luscious sauce. Asparagus is a great choice in springtime, but sautéed broccoli, cabbage, and kale are all good candidates, too.

INGREDIENTS

16 asparagus spears, tough ends removed

Extra-virgin olive oil for drizzling

Salt and freshly ground pepper

3 Tbsp butter

2 thin slices pancetta, finely chopped

1 cup (2 oz/60 g) fresh bread crumbs (page 251)

4 large eggs

Freshly grated Parmesan cheese for garnish

TOOLS

chef's knife, rasp grater, baking dish, small frying pan, large frying pan, slotted spatula

Preheat the oven to 400°F (200°C).

Spread the asparagus spears in a baking dish large enough to hold them in a single layer. Drizzle with oil and season with salt and pepper. Turn the spears several times to coat them evenly with the oil. Roast, turning once or twice, until the spears are tender-crisp and their color has darkened slightly, about 15 minutes; the timing will depend on the thickness of the spears. Cover loosely with foil and set aside.

In a small frying pan over medium-high heat, melt 1 tablespoon of the butter. When it foams, add the pancetta and cook, stirring, just until it darkens slightly, about 1 minute. Add the bread crumbs and cook, stirring often, until golden, about 2 minutes. Set aside.

In a large frying pan over medium-high heat, melt the remaining 2 tablespoons butter. When it foams, break the eggs into the pan, spacing them about 1 inch (2.5 cm) apart. Reduce the heat to low and season the eggs with salt and pepper. Cover the pan and cook until the whites are set and the yolks begin to firm around the edges, 5–7 minutes. Remove from the heat.

Just before the eggs are ready, divide the asparagus evenly among individual plates. Using a slotted spatula, transfer the eggs to the plates. Sprinkle the eggs and asparagus with the pancetta–bread crumb mixture, top with a light dusting of Parmesan cheese, and serve.

SERVES 4

SMOKED SALMON AND ARTICHOKE HASH

A good breakfast hash always has a wonderful mix of flavors and textures. Here, we use smoked salmon instead of traditional corned beef, which keeps the dish light; the sweet, smoky flavor of the fish nicely complements the hearty vegetables. Sometimes we reduce the richness by omitting the cream.

INGREDIENTS

½ lemon

6 artichokes, 10–12 oz (315–375 g) each

4 Tbsp (2 fl oz/60 ml) extra-virgin olive oil

1 red bell pepper, seeded and thinly sliced

1 yellow onion, sliced

4 Yukon gold potatoes, about 1¼ lb (625 g) total weight, cut into ½-inch (12-mm) dice

1 lb (500 g) smoked salmon, torn into ½-inch (12-mm) pieces

Salt and freshly ground pepper

½ cup (4 fl oz/125 ml) heavy cream

TOOLS

chef's knife, large mixing bowl, citrus reamer or press, large frying pan

Fill a large bowl three-fourths full with water. Squeeze in the juice of the lemon half. Working with 1 artichoke at a time, cut off the top ¾ inch (2 cm) of the leaves to remove the spiny tips. Snap off the tough, dark green outer leaves until you reach the tenderest, pale green inner leaves. Cut off the stem even with the bottom, trim the base, and then cut the artichoke in half lengthwise. Using a small spoon, scrape out the prickly choke from the center, and then drop the halves into the lemon water to prevent the cut portions from turning brown. Repeat with the remaining artichokes.

In a large frying pan over medium-high heat, warm the oil. Add the bell pepper and onion and cook, stirring frequently, until slightly softened, 3–5 minutes. Add the potatoes and cook, stirring frequently, until almost tender, 5–7 minutes.

Remove the artichoke halves from the water, pat dry, and cut lengthwise into thin slices. Add to the pan along with the smoked salmon, season with salt and pepper, and stir to mix well. Stir in the cream, reduce the heat to medium, and simmer gently, stirring occasionally, until the artichokes and potatoes are soft, 8–10 minutes.

Spoon into bowls and serve.

SERVES 4

APPLE AND SAUSAGE PATTIES

Adding shredded apple to bulk pork sausage yields flavorful breakfast patties that are a fresh alternative to store-bought sausages.

INGREDIENTS

1 lb (500 g) bulk pork sausage

1 tart green apple, peeled, cored, and shredded

¼ cup (1 oz/30 g) fine dried bread crumbs

2 Tbsp heavy cream

1 large egg yolk

Salt and freshly ground pepper

Canola oil for frying

TOOLS

paring knife, box grater, mixing bowl, baking sheet, large frying pan, spatula, ovenproof dish

In a bowl, combine the sausage, apple, bread crumbs, cream, egg yolk, ½ teaspoon salt, and ¼ teaspoon pepper and mix well. Divide the mixture into 12 equal portions and shape each portion into a patty ¼ inch (6 mm) thick. Arrange the patties on a baking sheet and refrigerate for 15 minutes. Bring to room temperature before cooking.

Preheat the oven to 200°F (95°C). Place a large frying pan over medium-low heat and coat with a thin film of oil. Place 4 of the patties in the pan and fry until browned on one side, about 3 minutes. Flip each patty and fry until browned on the second side, about 4 minutes. Transfer the patties to an ovenproof dish and keep warm in the oven. Cook the remaining patties in the same way, oiling the pan between batches. Serve warm.

SERVES 6

BACON WITH BROWN SUGAR AND CARDAMON

Nearly everyone likes bacon, but seasoning it with brown sugar and fragrant cardamom and baking it puts this breakfast mainstay over the top.

INGREDIENTS

1 lb (500 g) thick-sliced lean bacon

⅓ cup (3 oz/90 g) firmly packed light brown sugar

¼ tsp ground cardamom

¼ tsp freshly ground pepper

TOOLS

rimmed baking sheet, small mixing bowl, tongs

Position one rack in the upper third of the oven and another rack in the lower third, and preheat to 350°F (180°C). Line the bottom and sides of a rimmed baking sheet with foil.

Arrange the bacon slices in a single layer on the prepared baking sheet. In a small bowl, toss together the brown sugar, cardamom, and pepper. Sprinkle the mixture evenly over the bacon slices.

Place the baking sheet on the upper rack and bake without turning for 25 minutes. Move the pan to the lower rack and rotate it 180 degrees. Continue to bake the bacon without turning until dark brown but not quite crisp, 10–15 minutes longer. Using tongs, lift the bacon slices, gently shaking off the excess drippings, transfer to a paper towel–lined plate to drain briefly, and then serve.

SERVES 4–6

CRAB AND CORN CAKES
WITH SWEET AND SPICY DIPPING SAUCE

Corn pairs well with the crabmeat in these crispy cakes because it does not mask the seafood's delicate flavor. The easy mayonnaise-based dipping sauce, a heady mix of heat, sweet, and tart, is the ideal bright, bold accompaniment.

INGREDIENTS

¾ cup (4 oz/125 g) fresh corn kernels

1¼ cups (10 fl oz/310 ml) mayonnaise

3 Tbsp fresh lime juice

1 tsp Old Bay seasoning

Salt

1 large egg

4 slices soft white bread, crusts trimmed and cut into small cubes

¼ cup (1 oz/30 g) minced green onions, including tender green tops

1 lb (500 g) jumbo lump crabmeat, picked over for shells and cartilage

2 Tbsp chile-garlic sauce

1½ Tbsp honey

Grated zest of 1 lime

2 cups (4 oz/125 g) panko bread crumbs

Canola oil for frying

Lemon or lime wedges for serving

TOOLS

chef's knife, citrus reamer or press, rasp grater, food processor, assorted mixing bowls, baking sheet, large frying pan, spatula

DRINK NOTE

The delicate texture of crabmeat begs for the finesse of a sparkling wine. But corn forms a lovely marriage with Chardonnay, a specialty of France and California. The solution? Open a bottle of Blanc de Blancs, sparkling wine made solely from Chardonnay grapes.

Put the corn kernels in a food processor and pulse 3 or 4 times, until the kernels are broken up but still chunky.

Transfer the corn to a large bowl and add ¼ cup (2 fl oz/60 ml) of the mayonnaise, 1 tablespoon of the lime juice, the Old Bay seasoning, ¼ teaspoon salt, and the egg. Stir to combine. Add the bread cubes, green onions, and crabmeat and toss gently to combine. Cover and refrigerate for 1 hour.

Meanwhile, to make the dipping sauce, in a bowl, mix together the remaining 1 cup (8 fl oz/250 ml) mayonnaise, the remaining 2 tablespoons lime juice, the chile-garlic sauce, honey, and lime zest. Season to taste with salt. Cover and refrigerate until ready to serve.

Place the bread crumbs in a shallow bowl. Divide the crab mixture into 12 equal portions and shape each portion into a patty 1 inch (2.5 cm) thick. Gently coat the entire surface of each patty evenly with the bread crumbs. Place the cakes on a baking sheet, cover, and refrigerate for 30 minutes.

Place a large frying pan over medium-high heat and coat with a thin film of oil. Working in batches, gently place about 4 cakes at a time in the frying pan, being careful not to crowd them. Fry until golden on one side, 3–4 minutes. Flip the cakes carefully with a spatula and fry until browned on the second side, 3–4 minutes longer. Transfer the cakes to paper towels to drain briefly. Repeat with the remaining cakes, adding oil to the pan as needed.

Transfer to a serving platter and serve warm, with the lemon wedges and dipping sauce.

MAKES 12 CAKES; SERVES 4–6

2

DRINKS and NIBBLES

DRINKS *and* NIBBLES

For us, cocktail hour is a low-key and evocative time. Having friends over for great drinks and casual food is our answer to entertaining while still maintaining our busy lives.

Jordan Instead of devoting all day Saturday to shopping and cooking for a dinner party, we can buy a few bottles of wine, fix a platter of charcuterie, set out a bowl of olives and some nice bread with olive oil, and ask friends to stop by any evening of the week.

Christie My husband may say that the crowning achievement of his life was getting married, but we both know that, secretly, it's our bar. Comprised of over a hundred bottles collected from our travels, this collection of spirits is indeed a marvel. Absinthes from Switzerland; whiskeys from Britain, Kentucky, and Japan; exotic mezcals from Oaxaca; amari from Italy; liqueurs from southern France—this bar has it all.

Jordan When I think of good drinking food, I imagine an array of strong flavors and textures to balance the intensity of the beverages. Think salty, crunchy, briny, meaty, chewy, and creamy. Nothing too complicated. Simple food slows down the effects of alcohol while quickening the spirit of a casual get-together.

Christie Cocktail hour can be a trip down memory lane. A tart margarita reminds us of the little fishing village in Mexico where we spent a glorious week. A crimson Negroni takes us back to the hot, dusty alleys of Rome. As much as a well-made drink can stimulate conversation, it can also be its main topic. Every sip of a spirit we've collected activates our taste memory, which can be just as powerful as a photograph.

QUICK IDEAS *for* FINGER FOODS

By the time we both finish work, exercise, and head to the kitchen to figure out what to cook for dinner, we're ready for nibbles and a drink. Our snack food is usually vegetable heavy, and we like items that are easy to pull together, like antipasti, shellfish, and dips and spreads.

The best way to ensure that you choose healthful, tasty finger food to accompany your evening cocktail is to keep the nibbles on hand. On weekends, we often make a batch of hummus or ratatouille, so that when we are peckish and open the fridge door, our lighter, more healthful snacks are the first things we see.

HUMMUS CROSTINI
Top toasted bread with hummus + celery leaves + drizzle of olive oil.

RATATOUILLE SPREAD
Sauté 2 Tbsp olive oil + handful finely chopped eggplant + 1 red bell pepper, seeded and chopped + ½ yellow onion, chopped + 1 clove garlic, chopped; add minced fresh basil and spread on toasted bread or crackers.

MARINATED MUSHROOMS
Soak small mushrooms in ¼ cup (2 fl oz/60 ml) olive oil + 1 Tbsp fresh lemon juice + 1 Tbsp sherry vinegar + salt and pepper.

OYSTERS WITH MIGNONETTE
Mix white wine vinegar + fresh lemon juice + chopped shallot + sea salt; serve with shucked oysters.

CURED FISH PLATTER
Arrange sliced smoked salmon + cured white anchovies + cured sardines + capers + crème fraîche + rye bread on a platter.

QUICK IDEAS *for* SPARKLING COCKTAILS

*We like cocktails with a little effervescence from sparkling wine or soda water.
These sparklers are lower in alcohol than the classics, which is especially welcome on
weekdays, and the bubbles deliver a kind of spiritual lift. They are always festive.*

We cannot live without bubbles, and our refrigerator is shamelessly stocked with Champagne and other sparkling wines, beer, tonic water, and various other effervescent liquids. Our soda maker is one of our most-used possessions. Here are some of our favorite concoctions. Each drink serves one.

CAMPARI AND SODA

Combine ¼ cup (2 fl oz/60 ml) Campari + ice + soda water; garnish with orange slice.

KIR ROYAL

Combine ½ cup (4 fl oz/125 ml) sparkling wine + 1 Tbsp (½ fl oz/15 ml) crème de cassis; garnish with lemon peel.

TOM COLLINS

Combine ¼ cup (2 fl oz/60 ml) gin + 2 Tbsp (1 fl oz/ 30 ml) fresh lemon juice + 1 Tbsp (½ fl oz/15 ml) simple syrup + ice + soda water.

PIMM'S ROYAL

Combine ½ cup (4 fl oz/125 ml) sparkling wine + 2 Tbsp (1 fl oz/30 ml) Pimm's No. 1 + squeeze of lemon juice; garnish with cucumber spear.

CAMPARI AND SODA

Combine ¼ cup (2 fl oz/60 ml) Campari + ice + soda water; garnish with orange slice.

KIR ROYAL

Combine ½ cup (4 fl oz/125 ml) sparkling wine + 1 Tbsp (½ fl oz/15 ml) crème de cassis; garnish with lemon peel.

TOM COLLINS

Combine ¼ cup (2 fl oz/60 ml) gin + 2 Tbsp (1 fl oz/ 30 ml) fresh lemon juice + 1 Tbsp (½ fl oz/15 ml) simple syrup + ice + soda water.

PIMM'S ROYAL

Combine ½ cup (4 fl oz/125 ml) sparkling wine + 2 Tbsp (1 fl oz/30 ml) Pimm's No. 1 + squeeze of lemon juice; garnish with cucumber spear.

BLOODY MARY

Garnish your hair of the dog with your favorite vegetables, such as celery and radishes. Or, try pickles, *peperoncini*, or a skewer of olives stuffed with pimiento, blue cheese, anchovies, or chiles.

INGREDIENTS

1 lemon, halved

4 cups (32 fl oz/1 l) tomato juice

2 tsp freshly grated horseradish

2 tsp A1 Steak Sauce or Worcestershire sauce

2 tsp celery salt

1 tsp cayenne pepper

½ tsp paprika

Freshly ground black pepper

2 cups (16 fl oz/500 ml) vodka

Ice cubes

6 celery ribs with leaves

6 long, thin radish slices

TOOLS

chef's knife, box grater, citrus reamer or press, large pitcher, 6 rocks glasses or tumblers

Squeeze the juice from the lemon halves into a large pitcher. Add the tomato juice, horseradish, A1 sauce, celery salt, cayenne, paprika, and a few grinds of black pepper and stir until thoroughly combined. Add the vodka and stir to combine.

Fill 6 rocks glasses or tumblers with ice and pour the vodka mixture over the ice, dividing it evenly. Garnish with the celery ribs and radish slices and serve.

SERVES 6

MICHELADA

In Mexico, folks sometimes add tomato or Clamato juice (6 tablespoons/3 fl oz/90 ml per glass) to this popular spicy beer cocktail. For a bit more fire, use 2 dashes of hot sauce.

INGREDIENTS

Coarse sea salt

3 lime wedges

Ice cubes

½ cup (4 fl oz/125 ml) fresh lime juice

Worcestershire sauce

Hot-pepper sauce

2 bottles (12 fl oz/375 ml each) Mexican beer such as Superior or Bohemia

TOOLS

chef's knife, citrus reamer or press, 2 tall glasses

Pour a thin layer of salt onto a small plate. Moisten the rim of a tall glass with 1 of the lime wedges and then dip the rim into the salt to coat it evenly. Repeat with a second tall glass, using the same lime wedge. Put the glasses in the freezer to chill for at least 15 minutes.

When ready to serve, put several ice cubes in each glass. Add half of the lime juice and a dash each of the Worcestershire and hot-pepper sauces to each glass. Pour 1 bottle of beer into each glass, garnish with a lime wedge, and serve.

SERVES 2

MIMOSA

A classic brunch cocktail, this crowd-pleaser goes together easily, making it ideal for busy hosts. You can trade out the orange juice for peach nectar to make a Bellini, or for pomegranate or cranberry juice for a festive drink during the winter holidays.

INGREDIENTS

1 cup plus 2 Tbsp (9 fl oz/280 ml) fresh orange juice, well chilled

6 Tbsp (3 fl oz/90 ml) orange liqueur such as Cointreau, triple sec, or Grand Marnier (optional)

1 bottle (24 fl oz/750 ml) Champagne or other sparkling wine, well chilled

6 orange-slice quarters

TOOLS

chef's knife, 6 Champagne flutes or wineglasses

Put 6 Champagne flutes or wineglasses in the freezer to chill for at least 15 minutes.

Pour 3 tablespoons (1½ fl oz/45 ml) orange juice and 1 tablespoon (½ fl oz/15 ml) Cointreau, if using, into each chilled flute. Slowly fill the flutes with the Champagne. Garnish each glass with an orange-slice quarter and serve.

SERVES 6

CLASSIC MARTINI

Garnish this classic cocktail with a lemon twist: Use the large notch on a citrus zester or a channel knife to remove a strip of zest from a lemon so that it forms a pretty curl. Twist the strip over the glass to release the essential oils from the zest, then rest the strip on the rim.

INGREDIENTS

Ice cubes

¾ cup (6 fl oz/180 ml) gin

2–4 tsp dry vermouth

2 lemon twists (see note) or pimiento-stuffed green olives

TOOLS

2 martini or rocks glasses, cocktail shaker, citrus zester or channel knife, 2 cocktail picks (optional)

To serve the martinis "up," put 2 martini glasses in the freezer to chill for at least 15 minutes. Or, to serve them "on the rocks," fill 2 rocks glasses with ice.

Fill a cocktail shaker half full with ice. Add the gin, and vermouth to taste. Cover, shake vigorously for 20 seconds, and strain into the prepared glasses, dividing the mixture evenly. Garnish each drink with a lemon twist or with an olive speared on a cocktail pick and serve.

SERVES 2

SIDECAR

Throw a Prohibition party and serve this cocktail, one of the most popular of that era. Add more orange liqueur to sweeten, or more add lemon juice for a brighter, more acidic finish.

INGREDIENTS

Ice cubes

⅔ cup (5 fl oz/160 ml) brandy

2 Tbsp (1 fl oz/30 ml) orange liqueur such as Cointreau, triple sec, or Grand Marnier

2 Tbsp (1 fl oz/30 ml) fresh lemon juice

2 lemon zest strips

TOOLS

chef's knife, citrus reamer or press, citrus zester or channel knife, 2 martini glasses, cocktail shaker

Put 2 martini glasses in the freezer to chill for at least 15 minutes.

Fill a cocktail shaker half full with ice. Add the brandy, orange liqueur, and lemon juice. Cover, shake vigorously for 20 seconds, and strain into the prepared glasses, dividing the mixture evenly. Tie each lemon zest strip into a knot, drop each knotted strip into a glass, and serve.

SERVES 2

MEYER LEMON DROP

This chic cocktail is elevated by using vodka flavored with Meyer lemon extract. If you cannot find it, you can use either plain vodka or any citrus-infused vodka.

INGREDIENTS

Superfine sugar

1 lemon wedge

Ice cubes

½ cup (4 fl oz/125 ml) Meyer lemon vodka

2 Tbsp (1 fl oz/30 ml) orange liqueur such as Cointreau or triple sec

2 lemon twists (see Classic Martini, opposite) or lemon zest strips

TOOLS

chef's knife, citrus zester or channel knife, 2 martini glasses, cocktail shaker

Pour a thin layer of sugar onto a small plate. Moisten the rim of a martini glass with the lemon wedge and then dip the rim in the sugar to coat it evenly. Repeat with a second glass. Put the glasses in the freezer to chill for at least 15 minutes.

Fill a cocktail shaker half full with ice. Add the vodka and orange liqueur. Cover, shake vigorously for 20 seconds, and strain into the prepared glasses, dividing the mixture evenly. Garnish each drink with a lemon twist (tied into a knot, if desired) and serve.

SERVES 2

SUMMER ROSÉ SANGRIA

Using rosé wine and a mixture of berries and stone fruits instead of the more traditional red wine and citrus slices makes this sangria the perfect refresher for warm summer nights.

INGREDIENTS

1 bottle (24 fl oz/750 ml) Provençal rosé wine

1¼ cups (10 fl oz/310 ml) white cranberry juice

1 pt (8 oz/250 g) raspberries

1 pt (8 oz/250 g) blackberries, or 2 cups (12 oz/375 g) pitted cherries

1 nectarine, pitted and thinly sliced

1 white or yellow peach, pitted and thinly sliced

Ice cubes

TOOLS

chef's knife, pitcher, 6–8 wineglasses or tumblers

In a pitcher, combine the rosé, cranberry juice, raspberries, blackberries, nectarine, and peach. Stir well. Refrigerate until the sangria is chilled and the flavors have blended, about 2 hours.

When ready to serve, fill 6–8 glasses with ice. Divide the sangria among the glasses and serve.

SERVES 6–8

MOJITO

The crisp taste of the mojito comes from the perfect marriage of lime, sugar, and mint. Don't skimp on the mint; using enough of the herb is key to achieving the right flavor balance. Be gentle when muddling the ingredients. The goal is to bruise, not crush, the mint to release its essential oils.

INGREDIENTS

Juice of 1 lime (about 3 Tbsp/1½ fl oz/45 ml)

2 tsp superfine sugar

16 fresh mint leaves, plus 2 sprigs for garnish

Crushed ice

½ cup (4 fl oz/125 ml) light rum

Club soda

TOOLS

chef's knife, citrus reamer or press, 2 highball glasses, bar spoon (optional), muddler or small wooden spoon

Combine half of the lime juice and 1 teaspoon of the sugar in a highball glass and stir until the sugar has dissolved. Add half of the mint leaves and muddle by mashing the mint firmly against the bottom of the glass with a muddler or the back of a small wooden spoon. Fill the glass with crushed ice and pour in half of the rum. Stir again and top with a splash of club soda. Repeat with the remaining ingredients in a second glass. Garnish each drink with a mint sprig and serve.

SERVES 2

ROSEMARY GIN AND TONIC

The addition of rosemary adds a refreshing twist to this classic cocktail. To release more flavor from the rosemary sprigs, bruise them before putting them in the drinks. Thyme or lemon verbena can be used in place of the rosemary.

INGREDIENTS

Ice cubes

½ cup (4 fl oz/125 ml) gin

1½ cups (12 fl oz/375 ml) tonic water

2 sprigs fresh rosemary

TOOLS

2 highball glasses or tumblers, bar spoon (optional)

Fill 2 highball glasses or tumblers with ice. Add half of the gin and half of the tonic water to each glass and stir. Garnish each glass with a rosemary sprig and serve.

SERVES 2

MARGARITA

Some mixologists swear by Cointreau and some by Grand Marnier. Some prefer silver tequila and others gold. Simply put, there are lots of recipes for the beloved margarita. Experiment with different tequilas and orange liqueurs and come up with your own favorite version.

INGREDIENTS

Coarse sea salt

1 lime wedge, plus 2 lime slices for garnish

Crushed ice

⅓ cup (3 fl oz/90 ml) silver tequila

2 Tbsp (1 fl oz /30 ml) orange liqueur such as Cointreau, triple sec, or Grand Marnier

2 Tbsp (1 fl oz/30 ml) fresh lime juice

TOOLS

chef's knife, citrus reamer or press, 2 tumblers or margarita glasses, cocktail shaker

Pour a thin layer of salt onto a small plate. Moisten the rim of a tumbler with the lime wedge and then dip the rim into the salt to coat it evenly. Repeat with a second glass. Put the glasses in the freezer to chill for at least 15 minutes. Carefully add some ice to each glass.

Fill a cocktail shaker half full with ice. Add the tequila, orange liqueur, and lime juice. Cover, shake vigorously for 20 seconds, and strain into the prepared glasses, dividing the mixture evenly. Garnish each glass with a lime slice and serve.

SERVES 2

CRANBERRY GIN FIZZ

A dash of tart cranberry juice gives the standard gin fizz a colorful winter update. If fresh cranberries are in season, add a few to each drink for a garnish.

INGREDIENTS

Ice cubes

2 Tbsp (1 fl oz/30 ml) fresh lemon juice (from 1 lemon)

½ cup (4 fl oz/125 ml) gin

2 tsp superfine sugar

¼ cup (2 fl oz/60 ml) unsweetened cranberry juice

4 Tbsp (2 fl oz/60 ml) club soda

2 lemon slices

TOOLS

chef's knife, citrus reamer or press, 2 rocks glasses, cocktail shaker, bar spoon (optional)

Divide 4–6 ice cubes between 2 rocks glasses. Fill a cocktail shaker half full with ice and add the lemon juice, gin, sugar, and cranberry juice. Cover, shake vigorously for 20 seconds, and strain into the prepared glasses, dividing the mixture evenly. Add 2 tablespoons (1 fl oz/30 ml) club soda to each glass, stir, garnish with a lemon slice, and serve.

SERVES 2

SPICED HOT TODDY

A postdinner hot toddy hits the spot on a wintry evening. Cinnamon is the spice typically added, but we call for ginger and star anise for a more complex layering of flavors.

INGREDIENTS

1½ cups (12 fl oz/375 ml) apple juice

1 tsp honey

½-inch (12-mm) piece peeled fresh ginger

2 star anise pods

½ cup (4 fl oz/125 ml) brandy

Juice of 1 lemon

TOOLS

paring knife, chef's knife, citrus reamer or press, small saucepan, fine-mesh sieve, 2 heatproof mugs

In a small saucepan over medium heat, combine the apple juice, honey, ginger, and star anise and bring to a simmer, stirring to combine. Remove from the heat and stir in the brandy and lemon juice. Strain into 2 heatproof mugs, dividing the mixture evenly and reserving the star anise. Garnish with the star anise and serve.

SERVES 2

LEMON VERBENA LEMONADE

POMEGRANATE SPARKLER

Lemon verbena adds hints of floral and citrus to homemade lemonade. If you can't find it, substitute mint. You can also use honey in place of sugar, though you may need to add a few more tablespoons to achieve the ideal sweet-tart balance.

A number of the pomegranate syrups now on the market are not as sweet as grenadine, the best-known pomegranate syrup. If you cannot find one of them, use grenadine, but increase the amount of lime juice added to the shaker to ⅔ cup (5 fl oz/160 ml).

INGREDIENTS

8 fresh lemon verbena leaves, plus more for garnish

½ cup (4 oz/125 g) sugar

1¼ cups (10 fl oz/310 ml) fresh lemon juice

Ice cubes

2 lemons, thinly sliced

TOOLS

chef's knife, citrus reamer or press, saucepan, fine-mesh sieve, pitcher, 6–8 tumblers

In a saucepan over high heat, bring 2 cups (16 fl oz/500 ml) water to a boil. Remove from the heat, add the lemon verbena leaves and sugar, and stir until the sugar dissolves. Let steep for 10 minutes. Strain through a fine-mesh sieve into a pitcher, cover, and refrigerate for 30 minutes.

Add 4 cups (32 fl oz/1 l) water and the lemon juice to the lemon verbena syrup and stir well. Fill 6–8 tumblers with ice and divide the lemonade evenly among the glasses. Garnish each glass with lemon verbena leaves and lemon slices and serve.

SERVES 6–8

INGREDIENTS

Ice cubes

½ cup (4 fl oz/125 ml) pomegranate syrup

½ cup (4 fl oz/125 ml) fresh lime juice (from 4–5 limes)

1½ cups (12 fl oz/375 ml) sparkling water

Thin lime slices for garnish

Pomegranate seeds for garnish

TOOLS

chef's knife, citrus reamer or press, 2 highball glasses, cocktail shaker

Fill 2 highball glasses with ice. Fill a cocktail shaker half full with ice and add the pomegranate syrup and lime juice. Cover, shake vigorously for 20 seconds, and strain into the prepared glasses, dividing the drink evenly. Top each glass with half of the sparkling water, garnish with a lime slice and a sprinkling of pomegranate seeds, and serve.

SERVES 2

DARK AND STORMY

This cocktail, the national drink of sunny Bermuda, is traditionally made with Gosling's dark rum and Barritt's ginger beer, but other brands are fine. Be sure to use ginger beer, not ginger ale; the former has a much zestier flavor.

INGREDIENTS

Crushed ice or ice cubes

½ cup (4 fl oz/125 ml) dark rum

1½ cups (12 fl oz/375 ml) ginger beer

2 lime wedges

TOOLS

chef's knife, 2 highball glasses, bar spoon (optional)

Fill 2 highball glasses with ice. Add half of the rum and half of the ginger beer to each glass and stir gently. Garnish with the lime wedges and serve.

SERVES 2

MARINATED OLIVES

Don't stick slavishly to the olive varieties listed here. At the market, choose a mix of shapes and colors that look enticing. Do choose the ones with pits, however, as they have the best flavor.

INGREDIENTS

½ cup (2½ oz/75 g) Picholine olives

½ cup (2½ oz/75 g) Moroccan olives

½ cup (2½ oz/75 g) Niçoise olives

1 orange

1 lemon

Leaves from 2 sprigs fresh thyme

1 clove garlic, minced

1½ Tbsp extra-virgin olive oil

TOOLS

chef's knife, citrus zester, mixing bowl, sauté pan

DRINK NOTE

Olives are a masterful match with one of our favorite wines, the oft-overlooked sherry. Try a well-chilled Manzanilla or fino sherry, or, for a richer style, pour a crisp, dry amontillado.

Rinse the olives under cold running water and pat dry with paper towels. Put them in a bowl. Using a citrus zester, remove half of the zest from the orange in long strips and add to the bowl. Repeat with the lemon. Add the thyme, garlic, and olive oil to the bowl and toss well.

Just before serving, heat the olives in a sauté pan over low heat just long enough to bring out their flavors and warm them gently. Serve in an earthenware crock or dish with a small ramekin for discarded pits.

SERVES 6–8

in the kitchen with

MINDY SEGAL
and DAN THOMPKINS

Favorite drinks
Sour beer and red wine—Côtes du Rhône and big Zinfandels.

Divvying up kitchen chores
Dan butchers and cooks the proteins and I make all of the sides.

What makes a perfect dinner party
Six to eight people who all get along!

Favorite comfort food
Beans cooked in Dan's ham hock stock. We buy dried beans from Rancho Gordo in California.

Holiday meal fiasco
The first Thanksgiving we spent together Dan came to my family's house. He was completely distraught that my family didn't serve gravy with the turkey.

Favorite ingredient
Bacon—smoked, salty, cured bacon. We have bacon every day.

Helpful kitchen tips
Throw away plastic containers and use Ziplock bags for storage and freezing. And save all of your carrot, onion, and celery scraps for stock.

Setting the mood
We use tons of votive candles to make the space feel special and intimate.

SPICY ALMONDS

Toasting almonds fills the kitchen with a sweet, heady fragrance. These crunchy seasoned nuts make a great nibble, especially when paired with a chilled rosé, a classic Manhattan, or an ice-cold beer. They also make a great addition to salads.

INGREDIENTS

2 cups (10 oz/315 g) whole natural almonds

Salt

2 tsp extra-virgin olive oil

1 or 2 pinches finely ground red pepper flakes

¼ tsp garlic powder (optional)

TOOLS

mixing bowl, baking sheet, wooden spoon

Preheat the oven to 325°F (165°C).

In a bowl, combine the almonds with 2 tablespoons water and 1 teaspoon salt, tossing the almonds to coat evenly. Spread the almonds on a baking sheet and bake for 8 minutes.

Remove the baking sheet from the oven, drizzle the olive oil over the nuts, and mix with a wooden spoon to coat the nuts evenly with the oil. Sprinkle the red pepper flakes and the garlic powder, if using, over the almonds and mix to coat evenly. Return the almonds to the oven and bake, stirring once at the midway point, until browned and fragrant, 5–6 minutes. Let cool completely. The almonds will keep in an airtight container for up to 1 week.

SERVES 6–8

RADISHES WITH SEA SALT AND BUTTER

This simple trio of radishes, sea salt, and butter is a French classic. The slightly sharp flavor of the radishes is complemented by the creamy butter and the briny salt, a combination that primes appetites for the meal to come. If possible, use vibrant red, pink, and purple radishes; an artisanal butter—the whiter the better; and a flaky sea salt like Maldon.

INGREDIENTS

1 bunch radishes

Sea salt

4 Tbsp (2 oz/60 g) butter, cut into 4 equal pats, at room temperature

1 baguette, cut into slices ½ inch (12 mm) thick

TOOLS

paring knife, serrated bread knife, small mixing bowl, colander

Trim the radish tops, leaving a few of the leaves if they are pretty. Trim away and discard the root ends. Submerge the radishes in a small bowl of ice water for 10 minutes to crisp. Drain and pat dry.

On a platter or individual plates, arrange the radishes, a pile of sea salt, the butter, and the baguette slices and serve.

SERVES 4

BRANDADE

You need just three high-quality ingredients—salt cod, whole milk, extra-virgin olive oil—to assemble this popular Provençal spread. You must plan ahead, however, as the cod has to be soaked in water for a full day to leach out the excess salt, leaving just enough to flavor the mix.

INGREDIENTS

1½ lb (750 g) salt cod fillets

½ baguette, thinly sliced on the diagonal

½ cup (4 fl oz/125 ml) extra-virgin olive oil, plus more for brushing

1 cup (8 fl oz/250 ml) whole milk

TOOLS

serrated bread knife, large mixing bowl, assorted saucepans, pastry brush, baking sheet, wooden spoon

DRINK NOTE

Brandade marries opposites—strong and mellow flavors, creamy and solid textures—which means it is complemented by a variety of drinks. We like it with piquant wines, like a Spanish Albariño or a Greek Assyrtiko. But it also shines alongside a classic dry martini (page 68).

In a large bowl, combine the salt cod with cold water to cover. Refrigerate for at least 24 hours, changing the water 3 or 4 times. Drain the cod.

Preheat the oven to 350°F (180°C).

In a large saucepan over medium heat, combine the cod with water to cover and bring to a boil. Cover tightly, remove from the heat, and let stand for 10 minutes. Remove the cod from the water and discard the water. Let the cod cool until it can be handled, then, using a fork, flake the flesh, removing any errant skin and bones.

While the cod is steeping and cooling, arrange the baguette slices in a single layer on a baking sheet, brush on both sides with olive oil, and bake until golden, about 10 minutes. Remove from the oven and set aside.

In a small saucepan over medium-high heat, warm the milk until small bubbles appear along the sides of the pan, then remove from the heat.

In a medium saucepan over low heat, combine the flaked cod and half of the olive oil. Using a wooden spoon, mash the cod into the oil until blended. Slowly add the remaining oil and the warm milk while mashing constantly, and then continue to mash until the mixture becomes a smooth purée.

Transfer the cod purée to a serving dish or bowl and serve, accompanied with the baguette toasts.

SERVES 4–6

ANTIPASTO PLATTER

We put out an antipasto spread for almost every dinner party we throw because it's easy: we just set out prosciutto or other cured meats, cheese, olives, sometimes nuts or figs, and breadsticks, and let guests nibble as they like. The breadsticks can be baked a day ahead and stored in an airtight container at room temperature until serving.

INGREDIENTS

FOR THE BREADSTICKS

All-purpose flour
for dusting

½ lb (250 g) purchased
or homemade pizza
dough

Extra-virgin olive oil
for drizzling

Sea salt

1 cup (5 oz/155 g)
assorted marinated
olives

6–12 oz (185–375 g)
thinly sliced prosciutto,
preferably prosciutto
di Parma

6–12 oz (185–375 g) each
pecorino romano or
Parmigiano-Reggiano
cheese and a soft
cheese, such as Taleggio

6–8 fresh figs, torn
or cut in half

TOOLS

chef's knife, baking sheet, pizza wheel

To make the breadsticks, preheat the oven to 400°F (200°C). Line a baking sheet with parchment paper.

On a lightly floured work surface, roll out the dough into a 12-by-8 inch (30-by-20 cm) rectangle about ½ inch (12 mm) thick. Using a pizza wheel or sharp knife, cut the rectangle lengthwise into strips about ¾ inch (2 cm) wide. Working with 1 strip at a time and using your palms, roll the strip back and forth on the work surface until it is thin and rod shaped. Pick up the ends of the strip with your hands and twist several times. Place on the prepared baking sheet, pressing the ends lightly onto the parchment so the breadstick will hold its length. Repeat with the remaining dough strips. You should have about 10 breadsticks. Drizzle the strips with olive oil and sprinkle generously with salt. Bake until light golden brown, 10–15 minutes. Transfer to a wire rack and let cool completely.

Arrange the olives, prosciutto, cheese, figs, and breadsticks on 1 or 2 platters or a large board and serve.

SERVES 4–6

BURRATA WITH GRILLED BREAD
AND HEIRLOOM TOMATOES

Luscious *burrata*, which is a shell of mozzarella filled with thick, fresh cream and shards of cheese, deserves to be accompanied by the finest bread. Look for a midsized Italian loaf with a good crust and springy crumb. Do not cut the slices too thin. You want to preserve the bouncy softness of the interior to contrast with the crunchy grilled exterior.

INGREDIENTS

1 baguette, sliced on the diagonal

¼ cup (2 fl oz/60 ml) extra-virgin olive oil, plus more for drizzling

4 cloves garlic, halved lengthwise

About 1½ lb (750 g) heirloom tomatoes in a variety of sizes and colors

1 ball *burrata* or buffalo mozzarella cheese, about 10 oz (315 g)

Sea salt and freshly ground pepper

TOOLS

serrated bread knife, chef's knife, charcoal or gas grill or stove-top grill pan, pastry brush

DRINK NOTE

To heighten the textural contrast of creamy *burrata* and crunchy grilled bread, we usually pour something with its own lively texture, such as Prosecco, Champagne, or other sparkler. A zingy white, like Muscadet, Pinot Grigio, or dry Riesling, is also a good match.

Prepare a charcoal or gas grill for direct grilling over medium-high heat, or preheat a stove-top grill pan over medium-high heat.

Brush the baguette slices on both sides with the ¼ cup olive oil. Place the slices over the hottest part of the fire or in the grill pan and cook until golden and etched with grill marks on the first side, about 3 minutes. Turn and grill on the second side until golden, 2–3 minutes longer. Transfer to a platter and rub the top of each toast with the cut side of a garlic clove.

Depending on their size, thinly slice the tomatoes or cut into halves or wedges. Arrange the cheese, tomatoes, and grilled bread on a serving platter. Drizzle with olive oil, sprinkle with salt and pepper, and serve.

SERVES 4–6

ROASTED BABY ARTICHOKES WITH AIOLI

Roasting artichokes brings out their natural nuttiness and sweetness. Here, we pair them with aioli, a mayonnaise-based dipping sauce flavored with aromatic saffron and sweet-tart Meyer lemon juice, for a great spring dish. If you cannot find a Meyer lemon, use a regular lemon and add a dribble of honey to the sauce.

INGREDIENTS

1 large Meyer lemon

2 lb (1 kg) baby artichokes

¼ cup (2 fl oz/60 ml) extra-virgin olive oil

Salt and freshly ground pepper

Pinch of saffron threads

¼ cup (2 fl oz/60 ml) mayonnaise

1 clove garlic, minced

TOOLS

chef's knife, rimmed baking sheet, large pot, citrus reamer or press, assorted mixing bowls, colander

Preheat the oven to 425°F (220°C). Line a rimmed baking sheet with foil. Bring a large pot three-fourths full of water to a boil over high heat.

Halve the lemon and squeeze 1 tablespoon juice; set the juice aside. Fill a large bowl three-fourths full with water and squeeze the remaining lemon half into the water. Working with 1 artichoke at a time, snap off the dark green outer leaves until you reach the tender, pale green inner leaves. Cut off the stem even with the bottom, trim the base, and then cut off about ½ inch (12 mm) from the top of the artichoke to remove the spiny tips. Cut the artichoke in half lengthwise and drop the halves into the lemon water to prevent discoloration. Repeat with the remaining artichokes.

Drain the artichokes, add them to the boiling water, and cook until just tender when pierced with a knife, about 5 minutes. Drain well in the colander and let cool slightly.

In a bowl, combine the warm artichokes, olive oil, and a light sprinkle of salt and pepper and toss to coat evenly. Pour onto the prepared baking sheet and spread into a single layer. Roast until the artichokes turn brown on the bottom and edges, 10–15 minutes.

Meanwhile, to make the aioli, in a small bowl, soak the saffron in 1 tablespoon hot water for about 5 minutes. In another bowl, combine the mayonnaise, garlic, and reserved lemon juice and mix well. Stir in the saffron with its soaking water, mixing well. Season to taste with salt.

Remove the artichokes from the oven and let cool slightly. Arrange on a serving platter with the aioli and serve.

SERVES 6–8

CRAB DIP WITH CROSTINI

This retro and restorative hot-and-cheesy dip is reminiscent of the fare served at suburban lawn parties in the 1950s. It can be assembled in advance and baked just before serving, ideally with a strong classic cocktail.

INGREDIENTS

FOR THE CROSTINI

24 slices sweet or sourdough baguette

Extra-virgin olive oil for brushing

FOR THE CRAB DIP

1 cup (8 fl oz/250 ml) mayonnaise

1 cup (4 oz/125 g) shredded Cheddar cheese

8 oz (250 g) cream cheese, at room temperature

1½ tsp Old Bay seasoning, plus more for dusting

1 tsp Worcestershire sauce

Salt and ground white pepper

¼ tsp dry mustard

1 lb (500 g) lump crabmeat, picked over for shell fragments

TOOLS

serrated bread knife, box grater, baking sheet, pastry brush, large mixing bowl, silicone spatula, small baking dish or soufflé dish

To make the crostini, preheat the oven to 350°F (180°C). Arrange the baguette slices on a baking sheet and brush them lightly on both sides with olive oil. Bake until golden, about 10 minutes. At this point, the crostini can be cooled and stored in an airtight container at room temperature for up to 1 day.

To make the crab dip, in a large bowl, combine the mayonnaise, ¾ cup (3 oz/90 g) of the Cheddar cheese, the cream cheese, Old Bay seasoning, Worcestershire, ½ teaspoon salt, ¼ teaspoon pepper, and dry mustard. Beat with a fork until smooth. Using a silicone spatula, fold in the crabmeat, taking care not to break it up too much. Spoon the mixture into a small baking dish or soufflé dish and sprinkle with the remaining ¼ cup (1 oz/30 g) Cheddar cheese. At this point, the crab dip can be covered and refrigerated for up to 1 day before baking.

If the oven is not still on from baking the crostini, preheat it to 350°F (180°C). Dust the crab mixture with a little more Old Bay seasoning. Bake the dip until golden on top and bubbling around the edges, 15–20 minutes.

Place the hot crab dip in the center of a large, heatproof serving platter, arrange the crostini around the dip, and serve.

MAKES 24 CROSTINI; SERVES 8

CRUDITÉS WITH TZATZIKI AND ROASTED EGGPLANT DIP

We love Greece, where *tzatziki* and roasted eggplant dip are on almost every dinner table. Use the crunchiest crudités possible to scoop up the dips, as it is their firm texture that helps showcase the smooth silkiness of the sauces. Some versions of *tzatziki* call for garlic. Add some if you like, but be judicious, as it can easily take over.

INGREDIENTS

FOR THE CRUDITÉS

½ lb (250 g) mixed baby carrots

½ lb (250 g) French breakfast radishes

½ lb (250 g) broccoli florets

½ lb (250 g) cherry tomatoes

½ lb (250 g) Lebanese or Persian cucumbers, cut into spears

1 head Treviso radicchio, leaves separated

FOR THE *TZATZIKI*

1 English cucumber, peeled, halved, and seeded

1 lemon

2 cups (16 oz/500 g) Greek yogurt (made with whole milk)

2 Tbsp minced fresh dill

2 Tbsp minced fresh mint

Salt and freshly ground pepper

FOR THE ROASTED EGGPLANT DIP

2 eggplants, about 1 lb (500 g) total weight

Juice of 1 lemon, or to taste

¼ cup (2 fl oz/60 ml) extra-virgin olive oil, plus more if needed

1 tsp minced garlic, or to taste

½ tsp red pepper flakes

Salt and freshly ground pepper

¼ cup (1 oz/30 g) crumbled feta cheese

1 Tbsp chopped fresh flat-leaf parsley

TOOLS

chef's knife, paring knife, box grater, fine-mesh sieve, rasp grater, citrus reamer or press, mixing bowl, rimmed baking sheet, food processor

To prepare the crudités, trim the tops of the carrots to 1 inch (2.5 cm) and halve lengthwise. Trim the tops of the radishes to 1 inch (2.5 cm) and halve lengthwise (keep whole if small). Trim 2 inches (5 cm), if necessary, off each broccoli stem and discard. Arrange all the vegetables on a platter and reserve.

To make the *tzatziki*, using the large holes on a box grater, coarsely shred the cucumber. Place in a fine-mesh sieve over a bowl and let drain for about 10 minutes. Discard the liquid and squeeze the cucumber to remove any remaining moisture.

Grate the zest from the lemon into a bowl, then halve the lemon and squeeze its juice into the bowl. Stir in the shredded cucumber, yogurt, dill, and mint. Season with salt and pepper and refrigerate until serving.

To make the roasted eggplant dip, preheat the oven to 500°F (260°C). Pierce the eggplants in several places with a fork. Place the eggplants on a rimmed baking sheet and roast, turning occasionally, until the eggplants collapse and the skins blacken, 15–30 minutes, depending on their size. Remove from the oven.

When the eggplants are cool enough to handle, cut them open, scoop out the flesh, and discard the skin. Coarsely chop the flesh and transfer to a bowl. Add the lemon juice and stir in the olive oil, garlic, and red pepper flakes. Season to taste with salt and pepper and let cool.

Transfer the eggplant mixture to a food processor and process until smooth, adding a few teaspoons water or olive oil if necessary to achieve a good dip consistency. Taste and adjust the seasoning with additional salt, lemon juice, and garlic if needed. Transfer to a serving dish, sprinkle with the feta, and garnish with the parsley. Serve the crudités with the dips.

SERVES 4–6

in the kitchen with

AKI KAMOZAWA
and ALEX TALBOT

Go-to hors d'oeuvre for company

Jalapeño poppers. We learned our version
from a woman who worked for us in Colorado.
We split open whole jalapeños, stuff them with
a blend of cream cheese and mozzarella, wrap
them in bacon, and bake them at high heat until
crisp, tender, and gooey.

Maintaining kitchen bliss

Ask for help when you need it. It's easy to fall
into a rhythm and assume the other person
knows what you're thinking, but even after
years together we still manage to surprise
each other. Communication is the key.

Holiday meal fiascos

One year Alex put dill in the Thanksgiving
stuffing. Let's just say he never did that again.
Another year we made a sheet of homemade
marshmallows for the sweet potato casserole.
It was on the top rack of the oven, stuck to the
heating element, and turned black. Fortunately
we had a backup sheet.

Favorite comfort food

AKI: Angel hair pasta with butter and cheese,
a childhood favorite.
ALEX: A good cheeseburger.

Kitchen strength as a couple

Adaptability. Working in professional kitchens,
you learn to expect the unexpected and roll
with the punches. We can easily change our
menu if we can't find an ingredient or disaster
strikes in the kitchen.

CROSTINI WITH WHITE BEANS, GARLIC, AND TUSCAN KALE

Here, pungent garlic, creamy white beans, slightly bitter greens, and peppery olive oil combine to create an innovative topping for toasted bread slices. Look for crinkly, deep green Tuscan kale—also known as lacinato kale, dinosaur kale, and *cavolo nero*—in farmers' markets during the cool-weather months.

INGREDIENTS

FOR THE CROSTINI

16 slices sweet or sourdough baguette

Extra-virgin olive oil for brushing

FOR THE TOPPING

12 small leaves Tuscan kale, about ¼ lb (125 g) total weight

2 Tbsp extra-virgin olive oil, plus more for drizzling

1 clove garlic, thinly sliced

½ cup (4 fl oz/125 ml) chicken broth

1½ cups (10½ oz/330 g) canned cannellini beans, rinsed and drained

Sea salt

Red pepper flakes

TOOLS

serrated bread knife, chef's knife, colander, baking sheet, pastry brush, large frying pan

DRINK NOTE

Any crisp white wine is good here, though an Italian Verdicchio or Vermentino would be especially fine because it carries a cleansing hint of bitterness on the finish. Gin-based cocktails, such as the gin and tonic on page 72, have the flavor punch to complement the crostini, as well.

To make the crostini, preheat the oven to 350°F (180°C). Arrange the baguette slices on a baking sheet and brush them lightly on both sides with olive oil. Bake until golden, about 10 minutes. At this point, the crostini can be cooled and stored in an airtight container at room temperature for up to 1 day.

Preheat the oven to 400°F (200°C).

Cut away and discard the central rib from each kale leaf and chop the leaves coarsely. In a large frying pan over high heat, warm the 2 tablespoons olive oil. Add the kale and cook, stirring often, until it wilts and sizzles in the hot oil, about 2 minutes. Reduce the heat to medium-low, add the garlic and broth, cover, and cook until the kale is tender but still holds its shape, about 10 minutes.

When the kale is tender, push it to one side of the pan and add the beans to the other side. Simmer until the broth is mostly absorbed, about 5 minutes. Using a fork, stir together the beans and greens and coarsely mash until the mixture just holds together. Season to taste with salt and red pepper flakes.

Spoon a heaping tablespoon of the bean mixture on top of each of the crostini and drizzle with olive oil. Arrange on a platter or individual plates and serve.

MAKES 16 CROSTINI; SERVES 4

FAVA BEAN, GOAT CHEESE, AND MINT CROSTINI

Fava beans have a limited season and take a bit of prep work to enjoy, so pour yourself a glass of wine, put on some upbeat music, and start shelling. When you bite into one of these crostini and taste the nutty, mildly bitter flavor of the favas, you'll know the effort was worth it.

INGREDIENTS

FOR THE CROSTINI

24 slices sweet or sourdough baguette

Extra-virgin olive oil for brushing

Sea salt and freshly ground pepper

Ice cubes

½ lb (250 g) fava beans in the pod, shelled

5 oz (155 g) fresh goat cheese

2 Tbsp chopped fresh mint, plus small leaves for garnish

1 Tbsp snipped fresh chives

2 Tbsp extra-virgin olive oil

TOOLS

serrated bread knife, chef's knife, kitchen shears, baking sheet, pastry brush, large pot, assorted mixing bowls, colander

DRINK NOTE

Make a round of mojitos (page 70) to accompany these crostini, both of them heady with mint. Or, whip up a batch of tart-sweet margaritas (page 72) or lemonade (page 75). Wine drinkers should uncork a French or New Zealand Sauvignon Blanc or a citrusy Rueda from Spain.

To make the crostini, preheat the oven to 350°F (180°C). Arrange the baguette slices on a baking sheet and brush them lightly on both sides with olive oil. Bake until golden, about 10 minutes. At this point, the crostini can be cooled and stored in an airtight container at room temperature for up to 1 day.

Bring a large pot of salted water to a boil over high heat. Meanwhile, prepare a large bowl of ice water. Add the fava beans to the boiling water and blanch for 1 minute. Drain in a colander and transfer to the ice water. When the beans are cool, use your fingers to peel the tough skin off each bean. Set the beans aside.

In a small bowl, crumble the goat cheese. Stir in the chopped mint and the chives. Spread the goat cheese gently over the crostini and arrange a few fava beans on top of each. Drizzle with olive oil, sprinkle with salt and pepper, and garnish with a few mint leaves. Arrange on a platter or individual plates and serve.

MAKES 24 CROSTINI; SERVES 6–8

WATERMELON, MANCHEGO, AND SERRANO HAM SKEWERS

Here, sweet watermelon joins forces with slightly piquant Manchego cheese and salty, meaty *serrano* ham. Assembled on cocktail picks and finished with black pepper and olive oil, these unexpected skewers turn out to be great appetite sparkers.

INGREDIENTS

1¼ lb (625 g) seedless watermelon

½ lb (250 g) thinly sliced *serrano* ham

5 oz (155 g) Manchego cheese

Freshly ground pepper

Extra-virgin olive oil

TOOLS

chef's knife, cocktail picks

DRINK NOTE

In keeping with the Spanish flavors of this savory and satisfying finger food, we like to serve a bright and zesty Albariño or a Cava, a delightful sparkling wine that hails from Catalonia. A Portuguese Vinho Verde, light and slighty sparkling, is also a good match.

Cut the melon flesh away from the rind and cut into 1-inch (2.5-cm) cubes. Cut the ham into strips about ½ inch (12 mm) wide. Trim the rind off the cheese and cut the cheese into thin pieces to fit the top of the watermelon cubes.

To assemble the skewers, place a piece of cheese on top of a watermelon cube, and then top with 1 or 2 folded strips of ham. Secure each bite with a cocktail pick.

To serve, arrange the skewers on a platter, grind black pepper generously over the top, and drizzle a drop or two of olive oil over each piece.

MAKES ABOUT 20 SKEWERS; SERVES 4–6

DEVILED EGGS WITH WATERCRESS

This is our modern take on an old-fashioned favorite. Organic eggs boast buttery orange yolks, which yield a particularly handsome filling. The cool, refreshing tang of watercress and tart lemon zest tempers the natural richness of the eggs.

INGREDIENTS

6 large eggs

1 large bunch watercress

1 green onion, including tender green tops, minced

1 tsp finely grated lemon zest

3 Tbsp mayonnaise

Salt and freshly ground pepper

TOOLS

chef's knife, rasp grater, saucepan, mixing bowl

Place the eggs in a single layer in a saucepan. Add cold water to cover the eggs by at least 1 inch (2.5 cm), place over medium heat, and bring to a boil. When the water is at a full boil, immediately remove the pan from the heat, cover, and let stand for 15 minutes.

Uncover the pan and place under cold running water until the eggs are cool. Drain the eggs, peel, and cut in half lengthwise. Using the tip of a spoon, carefully dislodge the yolks, allowing them to fall into a bowl. Set the whites aside, hollow side up. Mash the yolks with a fork until very smooth.

Cut the tough stems from the watercress and discard. Mince enough of the watercress leaves to measure ¼ cup (⅓ oz/10 g). Add the minced watercress, green onion, lemon zest, and mayonnaise to the yolks and mix well with a fork. The mixture should have a smooth, creamy consistency. Season to taste with salt.

Arrange the egg whites on a serving platter. Using a small spoon, divide the egg yolk mixture evenly among the egg whites, mounding the mixture slightly in the centers. Grind a little pepper over the top of each stuffed egg, sprinkle lightly with salt, and serve.

MAKES 12 DEVILED EGGS; SERVES 4–6

TUNA TARTARE WITH SESAME

Don't shy away from preparing raw fish. Go to a fish market that carries sushi-grade tuna and work quickly when you are cutting the fish and this dish will be a success. The Asian flavors of ginger, soy, chile, and lime juice highlight the clean, silky taste of the tuna, and a scattering of sesame seeds delivers a nice crunch.

INGREDIENTS

2 tsp sesame seeds

1 lb (500 g) sushi-grade tuna fillet

¾ tsp peeled and minced fresh ginger

1½ Tbsp soy sauce, preferably reduced sodium

2¼ tsp fresh lime juice

1 jalapeño chile, finely minced

1½ Tbsp Asian sesame oil

8 pieces fresh chives, about 1½ inches (4 cm) long

TOOLS

chef's knife, citrus reamer or press, small frying pan, mixing bowl

In a small, dry frying pan over medium heat, toast the sesame seeds, stirring often, until fragrant and beginning to brown, 2–5 minutes. Pour onto a small plate to cool.

Using a very sharp knife, trim away any sinew or skin from the tuna fillet. Cut the tuna into ¼-inch (6-mm) cubes and place in a bowl. Add the ginger, soy sauce, lime juice, jalapeño, and sesame oil and stir gently to combine.

To serve, divide the tuna among individual bowls or plates and sprinkle the sesame seeds on top, dividing them evenly. Top with the chives and serve.

SERVES 4

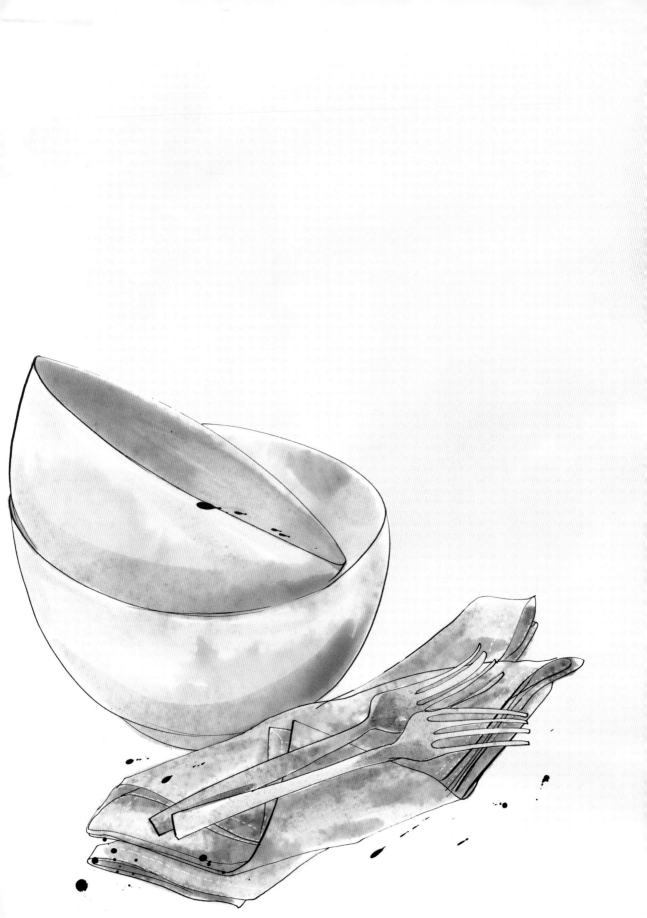

3

SUPPER for TWO

SUPPER *for* TWO

The intimate dinner for two is our shared DNA, and is the key to who we are as a couple. That's because we skipped casual dating—coffee, movies—and went straight to the kitchen.

Jordan Shortly after we met, I invited Christie on a date for what I believe is the most fun two people can have: cooking at home. Looking back, my ambition seems impossibly foolhardy and naïve. She was a New England–bred, suit-wearing, French-speaking, red-convertible-driving sommelier at one of the country's finest restaurants. I was from Texas, a bicycle-riding, underemployed freelance writer who lived in a flat with shag carpet and two hippie roommates. Simply put, she was out of my league.

My roommates made themselves scarce and I spent all day on the meal, deciding to fix rabbit, something I had never cooked. It seemed the perfect choice: sophisticated yet humble, earthy, and (I'd read) had an affinity for wine. Surely she'd be impressed, right?

Christie The hideous shag carpet in his apartment didn't bother me. I worked every night in a fancy restaurant and seldom cooked, so a home-cooked meal sounded great. I brought a couple of bottles of Burgundy and a Champagne, which we sipped on and flirted over until he revealed the main course.

I happily eat almost anything . . . except for rabbit. When I was a child, rabbit was sort of my spirit animal, my trademark. My parents' attic is still filled with my old rabbit memorabilia from those days. In other words, I couldn't possibly eat rabbit.

But I did. I forced myself, aided by lots of Burgundy. And it was good, and this new guy was both charming and a fine cook. That night went well, as did our next few dates, all of which were home-cooked dinners for two.

QUICK IDEAS *for* SALADS

We eat a salad at almost every meal because we just can't seem to get enough crunchy lettuce and vegetables tossed with flavorful dressings. We typically eat our salad after the main course in the French style, except on pizza night, when we have it alongside our slices.

Most great salads start with perfectly fresh lettuce or other greens, so we always look for the crispiest heads or most tender baby greens at the farmers' market or local produce store. Romaine or butter lettuce is often our starting point. We then toss hearty greens like chicory, frisée, and arugula into the mix, varying the combinations as we like during the week.

FRENCH-STYLE GREEN SALAD
1 head butter lettuce + ½ bunch fresh chives + shallot vinaigrette (right).

SPINACH SALAD
6 handfuls baby spinach + ½ red onion, thinly sliced + 2 handfuls sliced mushrooms + balsamic vinaigrette (right).

CRUNCH AND CHOP
2 romaine hearts, chopped + handful chopped celery + handful croutons + minced hard-boiled egg + lemon dressing or Caesar dressing (right).

ASIAN SLAW
½ head cabbage, shredded + 1 carrot, peeled and shredded + ½ bunch fresh cilantro, chopped + 5 fresh mint leaves, chopped + Asian dressing (right).

QUICK IDEAS *for* DRESSINGS

Dressings vary with our mood, but we like the tang of high acidity, which means we usually use some version of a vinaigrette. A little goes a long way—you don't want overdressed greens. Empty jam jars are perfect to use for making dressings. Store any extra in the refrigerator.

Sometimes we make the dressings right on the salad, tossing the various ingredients onto the greens. And sometimes we make the dressing in a jar, cap it, and shake vigorously until emulsified. If using raw garlic or shallots in the dressing, chop them, soak them in the vinegar or lemon juice called for in the dressing for 10 minutes to diffuse some of their sharp flavor, and then add them and the liquid to the rest of the ingredients.

DILL VINAIGRETTE
1 Tbsp white wine vinegar + pinch dried dill + salt and pepper + 3 Tbsp extra-virgin olive oil.

DIJON VINAIGRETTE
1 Tbsp Dijon mustard + 1 Tbsp white wine vinegar + pinch sugar + salt and pepper + 3 Tbsp extra-virgin olive oil.

SHALLOT VINAIGRETTE
1 shallot, minced + ½ Tbsp Dijon mustard + 1 Tbsp white wine vinegar + pinch dried dill + pinch dried thyme + salt and pepper + 3 Tbsp extra-virgin olive oil.

BALSAMIC VINAIGRETTE
1 shallot, minced + 1 Tbsp balsamic vinegar + salt and pepper + 3 Tbsp extra-virgin olive oil.

LEMON DRESSING
1½ tsp minced garlic + 1 Tbsp fresh lemon juice + salt and pepper + 3 Tbsp extra-virgin olive oil.

EASY CAESAR DRESSING
1½ tsp minced garlic + 3 anchovy fillets, minced + 1 Tbsp fresh lemon juice + salt and pepper + 3 Tbsp extra-virgin olive oil.

ASIAN DRESSING
1½ tsp minced garlic + 1 tsp peeled and grated fresh ginger + 1 Tbsp Asian sesame oil + 1 Tbsp rice vinegar + salt and pepper + 2 Tbsp canola oil.

GAZPACHO

Gazpacho is one of our favorite summertime dishes. Some like it chunky, but we generally purée it until it is fairly smooth and then throw in some croutons for crunch. Accompany it with salad for a light supper or with grilled shrimp for a more robust meal.

INGREDIENTS

1 lb (500 g) ripe tomatoes, seeded and cut into 1-inch (2.5-cm) pieces

½ cup (3 oz/90 g) canned plum tomatoes, with juice

1 large clove garlic, chopped

¼ cup (1 oz/30 g) seeded and chopped English cucumber

¼ cup (1 oz/30 g) chopped red onion

¼ cup (1 oz/30 g) seeded and chopped red bell or gypsy pepper

1 slice day-old coarse country bread, crust removed, torn into 1-inch (2.5-cm) pieces

1½ tsp sherry vinegar

1 tsp extra-virgin olive oil, plus more for drizzling

Dash of hot-pepper sauce

Salt and freshly ground pepper

FOR THE CROUTONS

1 tsp extra-virgin olive oil

1 slice day-old coarse country bread, cut into 1-inch (2.5-cm) cubes

TOOLS

chef's knife, blender, frying pan, airtight container

In a blender, combine the fresh and canned tomatoes and the garlic and process to a coarse purée.

Add the cucumber, onion, bell pepper, and bread and process until the soup is a fairly smooth purée. Add the vinegar, olive oil, and hot-pepper sauce and process until combined. Season to taste with salt and pepper.

Transfer the soup to an airtight container and refrigerate for at least 3 hours or up to overnight.

When ready to serve, make the croutons. In a frying pan over medium-high heat, warm the olive oil. Add the bread cubes and fry, stirring often, until golden on all sides, about 5 minutes. Transfer to a plate and let cool.

Taste the gazpacho and adjust the seasoning. Divide between 2 bowls and top each serving with half of the croutons. Drizzle with olive oil and serve.

SERVES 2

RED LENTIL SOUP WITH CRISPY ONIONS

The inspiration for this recipe comes from the richly seasoned lentil dishes popular in the cuisines of Egypt, Lebanon, and their neighbors. Red lentils cook more quickly than many other legumes, making this satisfying spiced-laced soup a good choice for a weeknight dinner.

INGREDIENTS

1 Tbsp extra-virgin olive oil

½ yellow onion, chopped

½ tsp ground cumin

¼ tsp ground coriander

Pinch of red pepper flakes

½ cup (3½ oz/110 g) split red lentils, rinsed

1 small carrot, peeled and finely chopped

1 small ripe tomato, peeled, seeded, and chopped

2 cups (16 fl oz/500 ml) vegetable broth

Salt and freshly ground black pepper

FOR THE CRISPY ONIONS

1½ tsp extra-virgin olive oil

½ small yellow onion, halved and thinly sliced crosswise

2 tsp fresh lemon juice

2 lemon wedges

TOOLS

chef's knife, colander, vegetable peeler, citrus reamer or press, saucepan, frying pan, blender or food processor or immersion blender

In a saucepan over medium-high heat, warm the olive oil. Add the onion and sauté until soft, about 5 minutes. Add the cumin, coriander, and red pepper flakes and cook, stirring constantly, until the spices are fragrant, about 30 seconds.

Add the lentils, carrot, tomato, broth, ½ teaspoon salt, and a few grinds of black pepper. Bring to a boil, reduce the heat to medium, cover, and simmer until the lentils fall apart and the carrots are soft, about 40 minutes.

While the soup is cooking, make the crispy onions. In a small frying pan over medium-high heat, warm the olive oil. Add the onion and fry, stirring often, until browned and crisp on the edges, about 15 minutes. Transfer to a plate.

When the soup is done, remove from the heat and let cool for 15 minutes. In a blender or food processor, process the soup until a smooth purée forms. (Or, purée the soup in the saucepan with an immersion blender.) Return the soup to the saucepan over medium heat, add the lemon juice, and reheat to serving temperature, stirring occasionally to prevent scorching.

Ladle the soup into bowls. Garnish with the fried onion, dividing it evenly, and serve with the lemon wedges.

SERVES 2

FATTOUSH SALAD

This riff on a classic Middle Eastern bread salad boasts sun-loving vegetables: juicy tomato, crisp cucumber, and a generous measure of parsley and green onions. You can use whole-wheat pita bread for a more healthful version, and add shredded cooked turkey or chicken to transform it into a light main.

INGREDIENTS

1 pita bread, 8 inches (20 cm) in diameter

1 ripe tomato, diced

¼ cup (1 oz/30 g) chopped green onions, including tender green tops

3-inch (7.5-cm) piece English cucumber, peeled, quartered lengthwise, and cut crosswise into ½-inch (12-mm) pieces

¼ cup (⅓ oz/10 g) coarsely chopped fresh flat-leaf parsley

FOR THE DRESSING

1 Tbsp pomegranate juice

1½ tsp red wine vinegar

1 Tbsp extra-virgin olive oil

Salt and freshly ground pepper

TOOLS

chef's knife, small mixing bowl, whisk

Preheat the oven to 325°F (165°C). Separate the pita bread into 2 circles. Place both pieces on the oven rack and toast until crisp but not colored, 3–4 minutes. Set aside to cool.

In a serving bowl, combine the tomato, green onions, cucumber, and parsley and toss to mix.

To make the dressing, in a small bowl, whisk together the pomegranate juice, vinegar, and olive oil. Season to taste with salt and pepper.

Just before serving, break the pita bread into 1-inch (2.5-cm) pieces. Drizzle the dressing over the tomato mixture and toss to coat evenly. Sprinkle the pita pieces over the top and serve right away.

SERVES 2

SPINACH SALAD WITH
POACHED EGGS AND PANCETTA

Spinach and bacon are a popular salad duo. Here, cubes of savory pancetta and a buttery poached egg provide a compelling update to the classic. The recipe takes advantage of the pancetta twice: the crispy fried bits are scattered over the salad, and the rendered fat becomes part of the warm vinaigrette that gently wilts the greens.

INGREDIENTS

2 tsp extra-virgin olive oil, plus more as needed

2 oz (60 g) pancetta, cut into ¼-inch (6-mm) cubes

3 Tbsp red wine vinegar

1 tsp fresh thyme leaves

Pinch of sugar

1 shallot, minced

Coarse salt and freshly ground pepper

2 large eggs

5 oz (155 g) baby spinach

TOOLS

chef's knife, small sauté pan, fine-mesh sieve, small heatproof bowl, assorted mixing bowls, wooden spoon, whisk, sauté pan, slotted spoon

In a small sauté pan over medium-high heat, warm the olive oil. Add the pancetta and cook, stirring occasionally, until browned and crisp, about 4 minutes. Pour into a fine-mesh sieve set over a small heatproof bowl, capturing the fat, and set aside.

In a small bowl, whisk together the vinegar, thyme, and sugar until the sugar dissolves.

Return the sauté pan to medium-high heat (it will still be filmed with fat). Add the shallot and sauté until soft but not browned, about 1 minute. Add the vinegar mixture, bring to a boil, and boil for 1 minute, scraping up any browned bits with a wooden spoon. Remove from the heat. Add a few grinds of pepper and 1½ tablespoons of the reserved pancetta fat to the pan, supplementing with olive oil if needed. Whisk until well blended to make a vinaigrette. Taste and adjust the seasoning, then cover to keep warm.

Pour water to a depth of 3 inches (7.5 cm) into a large sauté pan, add a pinch of salt, and bring to a simmer over medium heat. Crack each egg into a small ramekin and carefully slip it into the water. Adjust the heat so that the water barely simmers. Poach the eggs for 3–5 minutes, then remove from the water with a slotted spoon and place on a paper towel–lined plate.

In a bowl, toss the spinach with a pinch of salt and a few grinds of pepper. Whisk the warm vinaigrette to recombine, then drizzle about half of it over the spinach and toss well. Taste and adjust the seasoning.

Divide the dressed spinach evenly between 2 plates and top each serving with a poached egg. Drizzle each egg with some of the remaining vinaigrette and season lightly with salt and pepper. Scatter the cooked pancetta over the salads and serve.

SERVES 2

CLASSIC CAESAR SALAD

We can never get enough Caesar salad. We like it crunchy and tangy, so we use crisp romaine lettuce hearts, rather than the softer outer leaves, and tart fresh lemon juice, raw garlic, and anchovy fillets (not paste). If you decide to make extra dressing for using later, add the egg just before serving.

INGREDIENTS

FOR THE GARLIC CROUTONS

2 Tbsp extra-virgin olive oil

1 large clove garlic, crushed and finely chopped

¼ loaf day-old wheat or white coarse country bread, cut into bite-sized pieces

Coarse sea salt

FOR THE DRESSING

1 large egg

2 Tbsp fresh lemon juice

½ tsp Worcestershire sauce

1 tsp red wine vinegar

1½ Tbsp chopped anchovy fillets

1 small clove garlic, minced

½ cup (4 fl oz/125 ml) extra-virgin olive oil

½ cup (2 oz/60 g) freshly grated Parmesan cheese

Salt and freshly ground pepper

1 romaine lettuce heart, about ½ lb (250 g), leaves separated and cut into bite-sized pieces

2 oz (60 g) Parmesan cheese for shaving

TOOLS

chef's knife, citrus reamer or press, rasp grater, assorted mixing bowls, whisk, rimmed baking sheet, vegetable peeler

To make the croutons, preheat the oven to 350°F (180°C). In a small bowl, whisk together the olive oil and garlic. In a medium bowl, toss the bread cubes with the garlic-oil mixture and a pinch of salt. Spread the pieces on a rimmed baking sheet in a single layer. Toast in the oven, stirring occasionally, until the cubes are golden brown, 9–12 minutes. Let cool completely before using.

To make the dressing, crack the egg into a small bowl. Add the lemon juice, Worcestershire sauce, vinegar, anchovies, and garlic and whisk to combine well. Gradually whisk in the olive oil. Stir in the grated cheese and season to taste with salt and pepper.

In a bowl, combine the lettuce, croutons, and half of the dressing and toss well. Taste and add more dressing if desired (you may not use all of it). Divide the salad between 2 plates. Using a vegetable peeler, shave thin curls of cheese over each salad and serve.

SERVES 2

FARRO SALAD

Cultivated primarily in Tuscany and Umbria, *farro* is an ancient wheat species with a full, nutty flavor. The light brown grains are delicious in this salad with crumbled cheese, small, juicy tomatoes, and a lemony vinaigrette. Look for semipearled *farro*, which does not need to be soaked before cooking.

INGREDIENTS

½ cup (3 oz/90 g) *farro*

Salt and freshly ground pepper

1 Tbsp extra-virgin olive oil

1½ tsp fresh lemon juice

½ cup (3 oz/90 g) cherry or grape tomatoes, halved

¼ cup (1 oz/30 g) crumbled *ricotta salata* cheese

1 green onion, including tender green tops, thinly sliced

2 Tbsp shredded fresh basil

TOOLS

chef's knife, citrus reamer or press, fine-mesh sieve, saucepan, whisk

In a fine-mesh sieve, rinse the *farro* under cold running water and transfer to a saucepan. Add 1 cup (8 fl oz/250 ml) water, place over medium-high heat, bring to a boil, and add ½ teaspoon salt. Reduce the heat to medium-low so the *farro* just simmers, cover partially, and cook until tender yet still slightly firm and chewy, about 20 minutes. Remove from the heat and drain well in the fine-mesh sieve.

In a serving bowl, whisk together the olive oil and lemon juice until well blended. Whisk in salt and pepper to taste. Add the *farro* and toss well. Gently stir in the tomatoes, cheese, green onion, and basil until all of the ingredients are evenly distributed. Serve at room temperature.

SERVES 2

SPAGHETTI ALLA PUTTANESCA

Pasta sauce made from vine-ripened tomatoes picked at the height of summer is incomparably delicious. We like to buy a flat of locally grown tomatoes every summer and can them so that we can enjoy their sunny sweetness all winter long. Sit down to this simple dish for lunch, dinner, or a late-night snack.

INGREDIENTS

1½ lb (750 g) ripe tomatoes

2 Tbsp chopped red or yellow onion

½ cup (½ oz/15 g) firmly packed fresh basil leaves, coarsely torn

Salt

¼ cup (1½ oz/45 g) chopped pitted Gaeta or other Mediterranean-style black olives

2 Tbsp chopped, rinsed capers

2 Tbsp chopped fresh flat-leaf parsley, plus more for serving

½ lb (250 g) spaghetti

1½ Tbsp butter or extra-virgin olive oil

Freshly grated Parmesan or *grana padano* cheese for serving

TOOLS

chef's knife, rasp grater, paring knife, saucepan, mixing bowl, large pot, colander

Core the tomatoes and halve crosswise. Using your fingers, push out the excess seeds from the halves, then chop coarsely. In a saucepan over medium-high heat, combine the tomatoes, onion, half of the basil, and ¼ teaspoon salt. Bring to a boil, then reduce the heat to medium. Simmer, uncovered, for 20 minutes, stirring frequently to prevent the tomatoes from sticking to the bottom of the pan. Add the olives, capers, and parsley and simmer for about 1 minute longer. At this point, the mixture should be fairly thick. If it is still watery, simmer for about 5 minutes longer. Taste and adjust the seasoning.

Remove from the heat and let cool slightly. Taste and add more salt if necessary.

Bring a large pot of salted water to a boil. Add the pasta and cook, stirring occasionally, until al dente, according to the package directions.

Just before the pasta is ready, reheat the sauce until hot and remove from the heat. Stir the remaining basil leaves into the sauce along with the butter. Drain the pasta and transfer to a shallow serving bowl. Add the sauce, toss to combine, top with more parsley, and serve, passing the cheese at the table.

SERVES 2

MUSSELS STEAMED IN
BELGIAN ALE, SHALLOTS, AND HERBS

Many types of Belgian ales are on the market. For this recipe, which calls for steaming mussels in ale with thyme and garlic, we like to use a mild, not-too-bitter type. Don't skimp on the amount of bread you put on the table. You will want to swab up every bit of the delicious sauce.

INGREDIENTS

2 Tbsp butter

¼ cup (1 oz/30 g) finely chopped shallots

1 clove garlic, minced

½ tsp chopped fresh thyme

¾ cup (6 fl oz/180 ml) Belgian ale

1 lb (500 g) mussels, scrubbed well and beards removed

1½ tsp Dijon mustard

2 Tbsp chopped fresh flat-leaf parsley

Salt and freshly ground pepper

Crusty bread for serving

TOOLS

chef's knife, wide pot, slotted spoon, whisk

DRINK NOTE

Almost any light, unoaked white wine will do here, such as a Sauvignon Blanc, Chardonnay, Pinot Grigio, or Riesling. But the ale in the cooking liquid means that a fine German-style pilsner or lager would be fine, too, as would a cool, crisp martini (page 68).

In a wide pot over medium-high heat, melt the butter. Add the shallots and sauté until soft, about 4 minutes. Add the garlic and thyme and cook for 1 minute longer.

Add the ale and bring just to a boil. Add the mussels, cover, and cook, stirring occasionally, until the mussels open, 6–8 minutes. As they open, using a slotted spoon, transfer them to a warmed serving bowl. Discard any mussels that fail to open after 8 minutes.

Remove the pot from the heat and whisk in the mustard and parsley. Season the sauce to taste with salt and pepper. Pour the sauce over the mussels and serve at once with crusty bread.

SERVES 2

PENNE WITH SAUSAGE AND GREENS

This well-rounded bowl of pasta includes nearly everything you need for a satisfying meal. Just add some crusty bread and uncork a bottle of wine, and dinner is served. You can use any greens or herbs you have on hand in place of the arugula, such as Swiss chard, spinach, or flat-leaf parsley.

INGREDIENTS

½ cup (2½ oz/75 g) peeled and finely diced yellow-fleshed or waxy potatoes such as Yukon gold or creamers

Salt

½ lb (250 g) penne or small pasta shells

1 Tbsp extra-virgin olive oil

½ small yellow onion, finely diced

1 sweet or spicy Italian sausage, casing removed

1 small clove garlic, chopped

½ cup (4 fl oz/125 ml) Tomato-Basil Sauce (page 250) or purchased tomato sauce

Red pepper flakes

Small handful of arugula or red mustard greens

Freshly grated Parmesan cheese for serving

TOOLS

vegetable peeler, chef's knife, rasp grater, small saucepan, colander, large pot, sauté pan

DRINK NOTE

It comes as no surprise that Italian wine and food are natural partners—after all, they grew up together—but here is a nice reminder. This dish is made for Italy's classic Sangiovese-based wines like Chianti, Rosso di Montalcino, and Morellino di Scansano, which match the dish with fruit, acidity, and earthiness.

Bring a small saucepan of water to a boil. Add the potatoes and a pinch of salt, lower the heat to medium, and simmer until the potatoes are just tender, about 5 minutes. The potatoes should retain their shape without falling apart. Drain and set aside to cool.

Meanwhile, bring a large pot of salted water to a boil. Add the pasta, stir, and cook, stirring occasionally, until al dente, according to the package directions.

While the pasta is cooking, in a sauté pan over medium heat, warm the olive oil. Add the onion and sauté until golden, 5–7 minutes. Add the sausage and use the back of a wooden spoon to break it into small pieces. Cook until the pieces are no longer pink in the center, about 3 minutes. Add the garlic, tomato sauce, a pinch of red pepper flakes, and the potatoes. Taste and adjust the seasoning with salt and red pepper flakes.

Drain the pasta thoroughly, reserving a few tablespoons of the pasta cooking water. Add the pasta and the reserved pasta cooking water to the sauce. Toss well, taste, and adjust the seasoning with salt or red pepper flakes if needed. Fold in the greens.

Divide the pasta between 2 plates or shallow bowls and serve. Pass the cheese at the table.

SERVES 2

ZITI WITH ARUGULA PESTO AND CHICKEN

Here is a new take on an old favorite. We use arugula in place of basil to create a pleasantly peppery pesto. In this recipe, it is combined with pasta, chicken, and a little *ricotta salata*. Later in the week, the remainder can be used as sauce for fish or as a delicious spread for lunchtime sandwiches, wraps, or grilled panini.

INGREDIENTS

FOR THE ARUGULA PESTO

1 clove garlic

2 Tbsp pine nuts

2½ cups (2½ oz/75 g) baby arugula

¼ cup (1 oz/30 g) freshly grated Parmesan cheese

½ cup (4 fl oz/125 ml) extra-virgin olive oil

Salt and freshly ground pepper

½ lb (250 g) ziti

1 Tbsp butter

1 cup (6 oz/185 g) cooked, shredded chicken

¼ lb (125 g) ripe cherry tomatoes, halved

½ cup (2 oz/60 g) *ricotta salata* cheese, crumbled

2 Tbsp freshly grated Parmesan cheese

TOOLS

rasp grater, chef's knife, large pot, food processor, frying pan, airtight container

Bring a large pot of salted water to a boil.

Meanwhile, to make the pesto, in a food processor, combine the garlic, pine nuts, arugula, and Parmesan and pulse to chop finely. With the machine running, add the oil through the feed tube in a slow and steady stream. Season with salt and a few grinds of pepper. Measure ¼ cup (2 fl oz/60 ml) of the pesto and set aside for the pasta. Transfer the remainder to an airtight container and refrigerate for another use. It will keep for up to 1 week.

Add the pasta to the boiling water, stir, and cook, stirring occasionally, until al dente, according to the package directions.

While the pasta is cooking, in a frying pan over medium-high heat, melt the butter. Add the chicken and cook, stirring occasionally, until heated through, 3–4 minutes.

Drain the pasta, reserving about ¼ cup (2 fl oz/60 ml) of the cooking water. Return the pasta to the pot Add the chicken, reserved pesto, tomatoes, *ricotta salata*, and Parmesan to the pasta and mix well, adding as much of the cooking water as needed to loosen the sauce. Season with salt and pepper.

Divide the pasta between 2 plates or shallow bowls and serve.

SERVES 2

real couple stories
WHAT WAS YOUR FIRST HOME-COOKED MEAL AS A COUPLE?

Mindy and Dan

Grilled fish. We went to Isaacson and Sons together for the first time. We bought a small fish we hadn't eaten before, but it seemed interesting. Dan gutted the fish and it took two hours. He grilled it and it was awful. Really, really awful. We left and went out for dinner.

Lisa and Emmett

Emmett cooked and I brought flowers. He made a roasted sweet potato salad with watercress and pecans, chicken breast with ancho chile sauce, and a poached pear with chocolate sauce. That was a long time ago!

Molly and Brandon

We made dinner together on our first date. We cobbled together a salad from produce we picked up at Pike Place Market and ate it with some Mt. Tam cheese and a baguette. We started with gin and tonics, and at some point, Brandon had a dark beer. The details get a little fuzzy at that point.

Saukok and Jamie

We met on holiday in Spain and after we returned home I visited Jamie in San Francisco (I was living in New York). He knocked my socks off with a hamachi appetizer, crab cakes, and homemade apricot ice cream.

Julie and Matt

After we were married, Julie had the longer commute. Since I got home first, I'd usually prepare something quick like a seasoned turkey burger and throw together a simple salad with romaine lettuce, carrots, and fresh bell peppers. Before we had a couch, we used to sit on the floor for dinner.

Andrea and Mac

A shrimp and crab boil on Emerald Isle, NC.

STIR-FRIED SHRIMP WITH ASPARAGUS, LEMONGRASS, AND MINT

This easy stir-fry is all about the bright flavors of springtime asparagus, citrusy lemongrass, refreshing mint, and sweet, briny shrimp. Shrimp are perfect candidates for a stir-fry because they can be marinated and cooked quickly. But the same mix of ingredients would also be good with scallops or sliced chicken breast.

INGREDIENTS

½ lb (250 g) shrimp, peeled and deveined

1 clove garlic, minced

2 tsp peeled and minced fresh ginger

4½ tsp canola oil

Salt

2 Tbsp plus 2 tsp soy sauce

2 Tbsp rice vinegar

2 Tbsp white wine

1 Tbsp honey

1 tsp cornstarch

1 tsp Asian sesame oil

3 Tbsp minced shallots

2-inch (5-cm) piece lemongrass base, outer leaves removed, thinly sliced

½ red bell pepper, seeded and cut into strips 1 inch (2.5 cm) wide

½ bunch asparagus, tough ends removed, cut into 1-inch (2.5-cm) pieces

Steamed jasmine rice for serving

1 Tbsp chopped fresh mint

TOOLS

paring knife, chef's knife, saucepan or rice cooker, assorted mixing bowls, wok or deep frying pan

In a bowl, toss the shrimp, garlic, ginger, 1½ teaspoons of the canola oil, and a pinch of salt. Let marinate for 30 minutes.

In a small bowl, combine the soy sauce, vinegar, wine, honey, cornstarch, and sesame oil, and stir until the cornstarch dissolves. Set aside.

In a wok or deep frying pan over high heat, warm 1½ teaspoons of the canola oil. Add the shrimp and the marinade and stir-fry until almost cooked through, about 2 minutes. Transfer to a bowl and keep warm.

Add the remaining 1½ teaspoons oil to the wok and heat until hot. Add the shallots and lemongrass and stir-fry until fragrant, about 1 minute. Add the bell pepper and asparagus and stir-fry until tender-crisp, about 2 minutes. Return the shrimp to the wok, add the soy sauce mixture, and stir-fry until everything is piping hot and the sauce has thickened slightly, about 2 minutes.

Divide the rice between 2 bowls, top with the stir-fry, sprinkle with the mint, and serve.

SERVES 2

SOLE WITH LEMON AND CAPER SAUCE

Petrale sole has a sweet, mild flavor that pairs well with tart lemon, briny capers, and creamy butter. Seek out the freshest fish you can find, as its quality will shine through in this simple preparation. If sole isn't available, substitute any delicate white-fleshed fish, such as flounder, turbot, or sand dab.

INGREDIENTS

2 lemons

3 Tbsp extra-virgin olive oil

1 Tbsp capers, rinsed and patted dry

½ cup (2½ oz/75 g) all-purpose flour

2 Tbsp fine-grind cornmeal

¼ tsp cayenne pepper

2 sole fillets, preferably petrale, about 6 oz (185 g) each

Salt and freshly ground black pepper

4 Tbsp (2 oz/60 g) butter

½ shallot, finely diced

1 Tbsp chopped fresh chives

TOOLS

chef's knife, small frying pan, slotted spoon, sauté pan, wide spatula

DRINK NOTE

This simple classic calls for a wine with the same modest charm. A lemony Petit Chablis or Muscadet from France, a briny Vermentino from Sicily, or a crisp, aromatic Spanish Albariño would all work with the sole.

Preheat the oven to 200°F (95°C). Peel and segment the lemons with a chef's knife.

In a small frying pan over medium heat, warm 2 tablespoons of the olive oil. When the oil is hot, add the capers in a single layer. As they heat, they will open, lighten in color, and float to the top. After 2 minutes, using a slotted spoon, transfer the capers to paper towels to drain. Rinse out the pan and set aside.

In a shallow dish, stir together the flour, cornmeal, and cayenne. Season each fillet on both sides with salt and pepper and dredge the fish in the flour mixture, coating both sides and shaking off the excess. Set the coated fillets on a plate.

In a sauté pan over medium heat, warm the remaining 1 tablespoon oil. Add the fillets and cook, turning once, until golden brown, 3–4 minutes per side, using a wide spatula to turn the delicate fish. Transfer to individual plates and keep warm in the oven.

Return the small frying pan to medium heat and add the butter. When the butter melts, add the shallot with a pinch of salt and sauté until the butter foams. Reduce the heat slightly and continue to cook until the butter browns, 2–3 minutes. Add the lemon segments and swirl the pan to heat them through. Remove the pan from the heat and promptly spoon an equal amount of the lemon–brown butter sauce over each fish fillet. Sprinkle the fish with the chives and fried capers and serve.

SERVES 2

GRILLED SALMON WITH MISO GLAZE

Meaty fish fillets readily absorb the smoky flavors of the grill. Stoke the coals so they are nice and hot for salmon, which is best when seared on the outside but still moist and bright colored in the center. If the fillets threaten to overcook, move them to a cooler area of the grill to finish cooking.

INGREDIENTS

FOR THE MISO GLAZE

3 Tbsp white miso

2 Tbsp mirin or sake

1½ Tbsp light agave syrup or honey

1½ tsp firmly packed light brown sugar

1½ tsp soy sauce

Salt and freshly ground pepper

Canola oil for grill grate, plus more for brushing

6 green onions, trimmed

2 skin-on wild salmon fillets, each about ¼ lb (125 g) and 1 inch (2.5 cm) thick, pin bones removed

TOOLS

chef's knife, small saucepan, whisk, charcoal or gas grill or stove-top grill pan, pastry brush, spatula

To make the miso glaze, in a small saucepan over medium-low heat, whisk together the miso, mirin, agave syrup, brown sugar, and soy sauce until the sugar dissolves. Cook until slightly reduced and thick enough to coat the back of a spoon, 3–4 minutes. Season with salt and pepper. Let cool.

Prepare a charcoal or gas grill for direct grilling over medium-high heat and oil the grill grate, or preheat a stove-top grill pan over medium-high heat.

Brush the green onions with oil. Brush the salmon fillets on both sides with the miso glaze. Place the salmon, skin side down, over the hottest part of the fire or in the grill pan and cook, turning once, until etched with grill marks and caramelized on both sides but still rosy pink and moist in the center, 4–6 minutes total. During the last few minutes of cooking, cook the green onions directly over the fire or in the grill pan, turning often, until well marked and slightly wilted.

Transfer the salmon to a platter or individual plates, arrange the grilled green onions on top, and serve.

SERVES 2

CHICKEN CUTLETS WITH OLIVE–LEMON RELISH

In this Mediterranean-inspired main course, a rustic, heady olive relish bombards crisply breaded chicken breasts with big flavors. Any leftover relish will keep, refrigerated, for up to a week. A salad of sliced tomatoes and a helping of green beans dressed with olive oil and lemon juice are all you need to complete the menu.

INGREDIENTS

FOR THE OLIVE-LEMON RELISH

1 lemon

1 small clove garlic

1 cup (5 oz/155 g) pitted green olives

1½ Tbsp nonpareil capers

1½ Tbsp chopped fresh flat-leaf parsley

½ tsp anchovy paste

Pinch of red pepper flakes

¼ cup (2 fl oz/60 ml) extra-virgin olive oil

2 boneless, skinless chicken breast halves, about 6 oz (185 g) each

¼ cup (1½ oz/45 g) all-purpose flour

Salt and freshly ground pepper

1 large egg

2½ Tbsp extra-virgin olive oil

½ cup (1 oz/30 g) *panko* bread crumbs

½ tsp dried oregano

½ tsp dried basil

TOOLS

chef's knife, rasp grater, citrus reamer or press, food processor, flat meat pounder, assorted shallow dishes, large frying pan, slotted spatula

To make the relish, finely grate half of the zest from the lemon, then squeeze 1 tablespoon lemon juice. Turn on a food processor and drop the garlic through the feed tube to chop it. Stop the motor, add the olives, capers, parsley, anchovy paste, pepper flakes, and lemon zest and juice, and pulse to chop the olives coarsely. With the machine running, add the ¼ cup olive oil in a slow, steady stream and process until the olives are finely chopped. Transfer to a serving bowl, cover, and let stand while you cook the chicken.

Using a flat meat pounder, pound each chicken breast half until flattened to an even thickness of about ½ inch (12 mm).

In a shallow dish, stir together the flour, ¼ teaspoon salt, and ¼ teaspoon pepper. In a second shallow dish, whisk together the egg and 1½ teaspoons of the olive oil. In a third shallow dish, whisk together the bread crumbs, oregano, and basil. Dip 1 chicken breast in the flour mixture, coating evenly and shaking off the excess. Then dip it in the egg mixture, coating evenly and allowing the excess to drip off. Finally, coat it evenly with the bread crumb mixture. Transfer to a clean plate. Repeat with the remaining chicken breast. Let stand for 5 minutes.

In a large frying pan over medium heat, warm the remaining 2 tablespoons oil until very hot but not smoking. Add the chicken breasts and cook, turning once and adjusting the heat as needed to prevent scorching, until golden brown, 3–4 minutes per side. Using a slotted spatula, transfer the chicken to a paper towel–lined plate to drain briefly, no longer than 30 seconds.

Transfer the chicken to a platter, top each breast with a spoonful of the relish, and serve. Pass the remaining relish at the table.

SERVES 2

GRILLED CHICKEN BREASTS WITH
SAKE, GINGER, AND TOASTED SESAME

Salty, nutty, intensely flavored miso has a bold, almost meaty taste. In this recipe, it teams up with mirin and sake to make a savory-sweet Japanese-influenced marinade for lean, mild chicken breasts. Serve with spinach wilted in Asian sesame oil for an easy and healthful weeknight dinner.

INGREDIENTS

½ cup (4 oz/125 g) white miso

3 Tbsp mirin

3 Tbsp sake

1 Tbsp sugar

1-inch (2.5-cm) piece fresh ginger, peeled and grated

2 green onions, including tender green tops, finely chopped

2 boneless, skinless chicken breast halves, about 6 oz (185 g) each

2 Tbsp sesame seeds

Canola oil for grill grate

TOOLS

paring knife, rasp grater, chef's knife, mixing bowl, shallow baking dish, flat meat pounder, small frying pan, charcoal or gas grill or stove-top grill pan, tongs

In a bowl, whisk together the miso, mirin, sake, sugar, ginger, green onions, and 2 tablespoons water until well combined. Transfer to a shallow baking dish.

Using a flat meat pounder, pound each chicken breast half until flattened to an even thickness of about ¼ inch (6 mm). Place the chicken breasts in the miso mixture and turn to coat evenly. Cover and refrigerate for at least 2 hours or up to 6 hours.

While the chicken is marinating, in a small, dry frying pan over medium heat, toast the sesame seeds, stirring often, until fragrant and beginning to brown, 2–5 minutes. Pour onto a small plate to cool.

Prepare a charcoal or gas grill for direct grilling over medium-high heat and oil the grill grate, or preheat a stove-top grill pan over medium-high heat.

Lift each chicken breast half from the miso mixture and shake gently to remove the excess marinade. Place the breasts over the hottest part of the fire or in the grill pan, cover, and cook, turning the breasts 2 or 3 times with tongs, until they spring back when pressed in the center, about 8 minutes total.

Transfer the chicken to individual plates, sprinkle with the sesame seeds, and serve.

SERVES 2

GARLICKY CHICKEN THIGHS

We always buy locally raised free-range poultry because it's tastier and humanely raised. Here, we use it in a dish that requires a minimum of attention from the cook. Once you have browned the thighs and briefly cooked the aromatics on the stove top, the oven does the rest of the work.

INGREDIENTS

1 lb (500 g) skin-on, bone-in chicken thighs, trimmed of excess skin and fat

Salt and freshly ground pepper

2 tsp extra-virgin olive oil

2 Tbsp finely chopped yellow onion

5 cloves garlic, peeled but left whole

3 sprigs fresh thyme

1 bay leaf

2 Tbsp dry white wine

1 tsp white wine vinegar

TOOLS

chef's knife, ovenproof sauté pan with lid, tongs, wooden spoon

Preheat the oven to 325°F (165°C).

Pat the chicken thighs dry and season generously with salt and pepper. In an ovenproof sauté pan with a lid over high heat, warm the olive oil. When the oil is hot, add the chicken, skin side down, and sear until golden brown, about 4 minutes. Do not turn. Using tongs, transfer the chicken to paper towels to drain.

Pour off most of the fat from the pan and return it to medium-high heat. Add the onion, garlic, thyme, and bay leaf and sauté until the vegetables are just beginning to color, about 4 minutes. Pour in the wine and vinegar and stir with a wooden spoon to dislodge any browned bits on the pan bottom. Return the chicken thighs, skin side up, to the pan, cover, and place in the oven. Bake until the chicken is very tender, about 40 minutes.

Transfer the thighs to individual plates. Spoon the braising liquid and garlic cloves over the chicken and serve.

SERVES 2

THAI RED CURRY BEEF

This curry cooks in less than 15 minutes, making it the ideal dish for a busy weeknight. Purchased curry paste provides an instant flavor infusion, and lean sirloin cooks in just minutes in the simmering sauce. Start a pot of rice before you begin the curry, and you'll have dinner on the table by the time the rice is ready.

INGREDIENTS

½ cup (4 fl oz/125 ml) unsweetened coconut milk

2 Tbsp Asian fish sauce

1 tsp firmly packed light brown sugar

1½ tsp fresh lime juice

2 Tbsp peanut or corn oil

½ yellow onion, thinly sliced

½ green or red bell pepper, seeded and thinly sliced lengthwise

1½ tsp Thai red curry paste

½ lb (250 g) beef sirloin or tenderloin, cut across the grain into thin, bite-sized strips

1 Tbsp toasted and chopped peanuts

2 Tbsp slivered fresh basil, preferably Thai

Steamed rice for serving

TOOLS

chef's knife, citrus reamer or press, saucepan or rice cooker, small mixing bowls, wok or deep frying pan, slotted spoon

In a small bowl, stir together the coconut milk, fish sauce, brown sugar, and lime juice until the sugar dissolves.

In a wok or deep frying pan over high heat, warm 1 tablespoon of the oil. Add the onion and bell pepper and stir-fry just until tender, about 3 minutes. Using a slotted spoon, transfer to a bowl.

Add the remaining 1 tablespoon oil and the curry paste to the wok and stir-fry until fragrant, about 1 minute. Stir in the sauce, bring to a gentle boil, adjust the heat to maintain a gentle boil, and cook until the sauce begins to thicken, 5–7 minutes. Return the vegetables to the pan, stir in the beef, and simmer just until the beef is cooked through, about 2 minutes. Transfer to a serving bowl and garnish with the peanuts and basil. Serve at once with the rice.

SERVES 2

BRAISED SAUSAGES WITH BROCCOLI RABE

First, we brown plump fresh pork sausages over medium-high heat and then treat them to a long, slow simmer in ale that renders them meltingly tender. Everybody knows that sausages go well with mustard, which means that mildly bitter broccoli rabe, a member of the mustard family, is the perfect partner.

INGREDIENTS

2 fresh sweet Italian pork sausages, about 14 oz (440 g) total weight

1 leek, including tender green tops, halved and thinly sliced crosswise

1 large red bell pepper, seeded and sliced lengthwise

1 bay leaf

Salt and freshly ground black pepper

1 cup (8 fl oz/250 ml) plus 1 Tbsp brown ale or lager

1 tsp red wine vinegar

2 tsp extra-virgin olive oil

½ bunch broccoli rabe, about 6 oz (185 g), tough ends removed, coarsely chopped

1 small clove garlic, finely chopped

Pinch of red pepper flakes

TOOLS

chef's knife, sauté pan with lid, frying pan

DRINK NOTE

Sausages are a dream to pair with wine or beer. For lighter pork sausages, pour a white; German or Austrian dry Rieslings work beautifully. Beefy sausages are wonderful with fruity reds like Zinfandel, Chianti, and Syrah. And, of course, a match of sausage and beer—anything from pale ale to stout—is perfect.

In a sauté pan over medium-high heat, cook the sausages, turning as needed, until golden brown all over, about 5 minutes total. Lower the heat to medium, add the leek and bell pepper, and continue to cook until the vegetables have softened, about 3 minutes. Add the bay leaf, ½ teaspoon salt, ¼ teaspoon pepper, the 1 cup ale, and the vinegar, cover, and bring to a boil. Reduce the heat to low and simmer until the sausages are cooked through and tender, about 20 minutes.

About 10 minutes before the sausages have finished cooking, in a frying pan over medium-high heat, warm the oil. Add the broccoli rabe and sauté just until it begins to color, 2–3 minutes. Add the garlic and red pepper flakes and cook, stirring, for 1 minute more. Reduce the heat to very low, add the remaining 1 tablespoon ale, and cover the pan. Cook until the broccoli rabe is tender but still bright green, about 5 minutes. Be careful not to overcook.

Transfer the sausages to individual plates. Spoon the braising liquid around the sausages, pile the broccoli rabe on top, and serve.

SERVES 2

GRILLED PORK CHOPS WITH
CARAMELIZED PEACHES AND BASIL

This is a quintessential dish for warm nights. Sirloin chops are a little tougher than loin or rib chops, but their flavor is more intense. We pair them here with two summer staples: sweet peaches and fresh basil. Tossing the peaches with a little maple syrup before grilling helps them to caramelize, and a drizzle of balsamic adds a welcome acidic bite to the finished plate.

INGREDIENTS

2 bone-in pork sirloin chops, each about 9 oz (280 g) and ¾ inch (2 cm) thick, trimmed of excess fat

1 tsp extra-virgin olive oil, plus more for brushing

Salt and freshly ground pepper

1 peach, quartered and pitted

1 Tbsp maple syrup

Canola oil for grill grate

1 tsp good-quality balsamic vinegar

Small fresh basil leaves for garnish

TOOLS

chef's knife, pastry brush, mixing bowl, charcoal or gas grill or stove-top grill pan, tongs

DRINK NOTE

Pork chops match well with both reds and whites. The use of basil and peaches points toward a bright white with good acidity and fruit, such as a German Riesling. For a red, pick something lush and exuberant with red berry fruit. A Pinot Noir from California or Oregon is a great choice.

Let the chops stand at room temperature for 30 minutes.

Brush the chops very lightly with olive oil and season both sides generously with salt and pepper. In a bowl, combine the peach quarters, maple syrup, and the 1 teaspoon olive oil. Season with pepper, toss to coat evenly, and set aside.

Prepare a charcoal or gas grill for direct grilling over medium-high heat and oil the grill grate, or preheat a stove-top grill pan over medium-high heat.

Place the chops on the grill grate over the hottest part of the fire or in the grill pan and cook until etched with grill marks and golden, about 2 minutes. Move to a cooler part of the grill or reduce the heat and cook, turning once, until the pork is firm and cooked through but not dry, 3–4 minutes longer. Set aside on a platter.

Place the peaches over direct heat or in the pan and sear, turning with tongs, until the cut sides are grill marked, 30–60 seconds total.

Transfer the peaches to the platter with the pork chops and drizzle the chops and the peaches with the vinegar. Garnish with the basil and serve.

SERVES 2

fig leaves
cilantro root
seeds
pit
onion flower
cherry pits
watermelon seeds
ginger
mato
chastnut husk
51

in the kitchen with

ANDREA REUSING
and MAC MCCAUGHAN

Favorite home-cooked meal for two
Spaghetti with garlic and chiles.

Always in the fridge
Salami, anchovies, and pickles.

Favorite cocktail
A little muddled fruit—whatever is in season, maybe tangerine, blackberry, or muscadine grapes—icy vodka and a dash of bitters.

Tip for maintaining kitchen bliss
The cook doesn't have to clean. Much.

Lazy morning breakfast
Eggs baked in cream, toast, and hot coffee and fresh Satsuma juice.

Favorite kitchen tools
Ancient cast iron pans.

Go-to hors d'oeuvre for company
We like to serve amazing, thinly sliced ham—like Benton's or Edward's. It's easy to keep on hand and is always very appreciated.

On the table during mealtime
Treasures our kids collect from the woods or the beach—fresh moss, nuts, pods, starfish, and rocks.

QUINOA TABBOULEH

The trio of green onion, parsley, and mint brings an abundance of bold herbal flavor to this Middle Eastern–inspired salad, which uses a South American grain in place of the usual bulgur. Quinoa provides the perfect earthy canvas for the summery vegetables and the dressing of fruity olive oil and tangy-sweet pomegranate molasses.

INGREDIENTS

¾ cup (4½ oz/140 g) quinoa, rinsed and drained

1½ cups (12 fl oz/375 ml) chicken or vegetable broth, or water

Salt and freshly ground pepper

1 large lemon

1 clove garlic, minced

1½ tsp pomegranate molasses

½ tsp sugar

¼ cup (2 fl oz/60 ml) extra-virgin olive oil

1 large ripe tomato, seeded and cut into ½-inch (12-mm) dice

½ small English cucumber, cut into ½-inch (12-mm) dice

2 green onions, including tender green tops, thinly sliced

2 Tbsp coarsely chopped fresh flat-leaf parsley

2 Tbsp coarsely chopped fresh mint

TOOLS

fine-mesh sieve, chef's knife, saucepan, assorted mixing bowls, rasp grater, citrus reamer or press, whisk

In a saucepan over high heat, combine the quinoa, broth, and a pinch of salt and bring to a boil. Cover, reduce the heat to medium-low, and simmer until all of the liquid has been absorbed and the quinoa is tender, about 12 minutes. Immediately transfer the quinoa to a fine-mesh sieve and rinse under cold running water until cooled, 1–2 minutes. Drain well, then transfer to a bowl.

Finely grate half of the zest from the lemon and then squeeze 2½ tablespoons juice. In a small bowl, whisk together the lemon zest and juice, garlic, pomegranate molasses, sugar, ¼ teaspoon salt, and a few grinds of pepper until the sugar dissolves. Slowly whisk in the olive oil until well blended to make a dressing. Taste and adjust the seasoning. Add about three-fourths of the dressing to the quinoa and stir well.

Add the tomato, cucumber, green onions, a generous pinch of salt, and the remaining dressing to the quinoa and toss to mix well. Stir in the parsley and mint. Taste and adjust the seasoning and serve.

SERVES 2

POLENTA WITH VEGETABLE RAGOUT

Creamy polenta makes the ideal bed for spoonfuls of this tomato ragout studded with mushrooms and summer squash. Quick-cooking polenta is available in most well-stocked markets. If you can't find it, use regular polenta and cook it for 25–30 minutes, or use cornmeal and cook it for 15–20 minutes.

INGREDIENTS

2 Tbsp extra-virgin olive oil

½ yellow onion, chopped

2 small cloves garlic, finely chopped

½ zucchini, sliced

½ lb (250 g) mixed wild and cultivated fresh mushrooms, sliced

¼ lb (125 g) ripe plum tomatoes, seeded and chopped

1½ tsp minced fresh rosemary

2 Tbsp Marsala, sherry, or sherry vinegar

Salt and freshly ground pepper

2 cups (16 fl oz/500 ml) vegetable or chicken broth

½ cup (3½ oz/105 g) quick-cooking polenta

2 Tbsp freshly grated Parmesan cheese

TOOLS

chef's knife, rasp grater, frying pan, saucepan, whisk

In a frying pan over medium heat, warm 1½ tablespoons of the oil. Add the onion and sauté until soft, about 4 minutes. Add the garlic, zucchini, and mushrooms and cook, stirring occasionally, until the vegetables are soft, 4–5 minutes. Add the tomatoes, rosemary, Marsala, ½ teaspoon salt, and a few grinds of pepper. Continue to cook, stirring frequently, until the tomatoes release their juices and are softened, 3–4 minutes.

Meanwhile, in a saucepan over high heat, bring the broth to a boil. Whisk in the polenta and ½ teaspoon salt. Reduce the heat to low and cook, stirring frequently, until the polenta is thick and creamy, about 5 minutes. Remove from the heat and stir in the remaining 1½ teaspoons oil and the cheese.

Spoon the polenta into shallow bowls, top with the ragout, and serve.

SERVES 2

MOROCCAN LAMB BURGERS

Reimagine burger nights with a Middle Eastern flair that features flavorful lamb, fresh herbs, and warm spices. A cool yogurt sauce and summery tomatoes and cucumbers make the perfect accompaniments. Toast the pita rounds on the grill, and serve the burgers on a bed of Quinoa Tabbouleh (page 136), if you like.

INGREDIENTS

Canola oil for grill grate

¾ lb (375 g) lean ground lamb

2½ Tbsp minced fresh mint

2½ Tbsp minced fresh flat-leaf parsley

½ small yellow onion, finely chopped

¾ tsp ground cumin

¼ tsp ground cinnamon

Salt

Cayenne pepper

¼ cup (2 oz/60 g) plain yogurt

½ cup (2 oz/60 g) ripe cherry tomatoes, halved

1 small cucumber, cut into spears

2 pita breads, grilled, if desired, and torn into pieces

TOOLS

chef's knife, charcoal or gas grill or stove-top grill pan, assorted mixing bowls

Prepare a charcoal or gas grill for direct grilling over high heat and oil the grill grate, or preheat a stove-top grill pan over medium-high heat.

In a bowl, using your hands, mix together the lamb, 2 tablespoons each of the mint and parsley, the onion, ½ teaspoon of the cumin, the cinnamon, ¼ teaspoon salt, and a pinch of cayenne pepper. Form the lamb mixture into 2 patties.

In a small bowl, stir together the yogurt, the remaining 1½ teaspoons each mint and parsley, and the remaining ¼ teaspoon cumin. Season to taste with salt and cayenne pepper. Set aside.

Place the lamb patties on the grill grate over the hottest part of the fire or in the grill pan and cook, turning once, until evenly etched with grill marks on both sides, about 10 minutes total for medium, or until done to your liking.

Place the burgers on dinner plates. Top each burger with a spoonful of the yogurt sauce and half of the tomatoes and place the cucumber spears alongside. Pass the remaining yogurt sauce and the pita bread at the table.

SERVES 2

SWISS CHARD WITH RAISINS AND PINE NUTS

Hearty and healthful Swiss chard is sautéed quickly with just a handful of ingredients in this simple side. The natural sweetness of the chard is complemented by the flavors of the raisins and butter. If you cannot find chard at the market, kale or spinach can substitute.

INGREDIENTS

1 Tbsp pine nuts

¾ lb (375 g) Swiss chard, tough stems trimmed

Salt and freshly ground pepper

1 Tbsp butter

1 Tbsp raisins

TOOLS

chef's knife, small frying pan, saucepan, colander

In a small, dry frying pan over medium heat, toast the pine nuts, shaking the pan often, until golden, about 3 minutes. Pour onto a small plate to cool.

Cut the chard crosswise into strips 1 inch (2.5 cm) wide. In a saucepan over medium heat, combine the chard, ¼ cup (2 fl oz/60 ml) water, and about 1 teaspoon salt. Cover and cook, uncovering to stir once or twice, until wilted and tender, about 5 minutes. Drain well in a colander, pressing out any excess moisture with the back of a spoon.

Rinse out the saucepan, add the butter, and set over low heat. When the butter melts, add the chard and raisins and cook, stirring occasionally, until the chard and raisins are coated with the butter and the flavors are blended, about 5 minutes. Season to taste with salt and pepper.

Transfer to a serving dish, sprinkle with the pine nuts, and serve.

SERVES 2

ASPARAGUS WITH LEMON AND PARMESAN

Salty, nutty-tasting Parmesan provides a sharp contrast to the acidity of lemon and the grassiness of asparagus. Extra-virgin olive oil, preferably a fruity one, nicely binds together all of the ingredients in this side. Any leftovers would be delicious tossed with salad greens for lunch or mixed into a frittata.

INGREDIENTS

Salt and freshly ground pepper

Ice cubes

½ bunch pencil-thin asparagus

1 lemon

2 tsp extra-virgin olive oil

2 oz (60 g) Parmesan cheese for shaving

TOOLS

large saucepan, assorted mixing bowls, chef's knife, rasp grater, citrus reamer or press, colander, whisk, vegetable peeler

Bring a large saucepan of salted water to a boil. Fill a large bowl with ice water.

Trim off the tough ends of the asparagus spears and cut the spears into 1½-inch (4-cm) lengths. Finely grate 1½ teaspoons zest from the lemon and then squeeze 1½ teaspoons juice. Set the zest and juice aside in a small bowl.

Add the asparagus pieces to the boiling water and cook until the asparagus is tender-crisp and bright green, about 2½ minutes. Drain and immediately transfer the asparagus to the ice water. Let stand until cool, about 2 minutes, then drain again. Transfer the asparagus pieces to a serving platter.

Add a pinch each of salt and pepper to the lemon zest and juice and whisk together. Slowly whisk in the olive oil until well blended to make a dressing. Taste and adjust the seasoning. Drizzle the dressing evenly over the asparagus. Using a vegetable peeler, shave thin curls of the cheese over the asparagus and serve.

SERVES 2

STRAWBERRY SHORTCAKES

Tart berries paired with sweet cream and tender biscuits epitomize summer. Make the shortcake dough a couple of hours in advance, pat it out, and refrigerate it until you are ready to bake. You can replace the berries with any other summer fruits that appeal to you, like peaches or nectarines, or a combination of berries and stone fruits.

INGREDIENTS

FOR THE STRAWBERRIES

1 cup (4 oz/125 g) very ripe strawberries, hulled and cut lengthwise into quarters

1 Tbsp plus 1 tsp granulated sugar

¼ cup (2 fl oz/60 ml) fresh orange juice

¾ tsp orange blossom water (optional)

FOR THE SHORTCAKES

⅔ cup (3½ oz/105 g) all-purpose flour, plus more for dusting

1 Tbsp granulated sugar

1 tsp baking powder

Pinch of salt

2 Tbsp cold salted butter, cut into small pieces

⅓ cup (3 fl oz/80 ml) plus 1 tsp heavy cream

½ cup (4 fl oz/125 ml) cold heavy cream

Dash of vanilla extract

1 tsp confectioners' sugar, plus more for dusting (optional)

TOOLS

paring knife, citrus reamer or press, 3 mixing bowls, wooden spoon, sharp knife, baking sheet, pastry brush, wire rack, whisk or electric mixer, fine-mesh sieve (optional)

To prepare the strawberries, in a bowl, toss together the strawberries, granulated sugar, orange juice, and orange blossom water, if using. Let sit for 30 minutes, stirring occasionally.

To make the shortcakes, preheat the oven to 375°F (190°C). In a bowl, stir together the flour, granulated sugar, baking powder, and salt. Using a pastry blender or 2 knives, cut in the butter until it is broken down into unevenly sized pieces, the largest as big as a pea. Pour in the ⅓ cup cream and mix quickly with a wooden spoon just until the dough starts to come together. The dough should look and feel sticky in spots. Turn the dough out onto a lightly floured, cool work surface. Dust the top lightly with flour and, using your hands, pat the dough out into a rectangle about 1 inch (2.5 cm) thick. Using a sharp knife, cut the rectangle into 2 squares. Place the squares at least 2 inches (5 cm) apart on a baking sheet and brush the tops with the remaining 1 teaspoon cream. Bake until risen and golden, 20–25 minutes. Transfer to a wire rack and let cool briefly.

Meanwhile, in a bowl, using a whisk or an electric mixer on medium-low speed, whip the ½ cup cream, the vanilla, and the confectioners' sugar until soft peaks form. Cover and refrigerate until needed.

To serve, split each biscuit in half horizontally and place the bottom half on a dessert plate. Spoon the strawberries and their juices on top. Place a dollop of whipped cream on top of the berries and top with the other half of the biscuit. If desired, using a fine-mesh sieve, dust with confectioners' sugar and serve.

SERVES 2

GRILLED BALSAMIC-GLAZED PLUMS

Grilled stone fruits can do double duty. They are as delicious served atop grilled meats (see page 133) as they are alongside ice cream for dessert, as presented here. Balsamic vinegar is both sweet and savory and reduces to a flavorful glaze when exposed to the heat of the grill. Other summer stone fruits, such as peaches, nectarines, or apricots, can also be prepared this way.

INGREDIENTS

Canola oil for grill grate

4 plums or Pluots, halved and pitted

2 Tbsp balsamic vinegar, plus more for drizzling

Vanilla ice cream for serving

TOOLS

chef's knife, charcoal or gas grill or stove-top grill pan, pastry brush

Prepare a charcoal or gas grill for direct grilling over medium heat and oil the grill grate, or preheat a stove-top grill pan over medium heat. Brush the plums on both sides with about 1½ tablespoons of the vinegar.

Place the plums, cut sides down, on the grill grate over the hottest part of the fire or in the grill pan. Grill, turning once and brushing 2 or 3 times with the remaining 1½ teaspoons vinegar, until tender and lightly charred, 5–10 minutes, depending on the ripeness of the fruit.

Transfer the plums to individual bowls or plates. Arrange scoops of ice cream alongside, drizzle with balsamic vinegar, and serve.

SERVES 2

CANTALOUPE GRANITA

Flaky, icy granita makes a light, refreshing finish for any meal. Make sure the cantaloupe is ripe: it should smell sweet and the stem end should give slightly when pressed.

INGREDIENTS

¼ cup (2 oz/60 g) sugar

5 ice cubes

½ cantaloupe, peeled, seeded, and cut into pieces (about 2 cups/ 12 oz/375 g)

3 Tbsp fresh lemon juice

TOOLS

chef's knife, citrus reamer or press, small saucepan, heatproof mixing bowl, food processor, 9-inch (23-cm) square pan or heavy dish

In a small saucepan over medium-high heat, combine the sugar with ½ cup (4 fl oz/125 ml) water and heat, stirring occasionally, until the sugar dissolves, about 3 minutes. Remove from the heat, pour into a heatproof bowl, and stir in the ice cubes. Continue stirring until the sugar syrup is cold, about 1 minute. Discard any ice that is not melted.

In a food processor, combine the cantaloupe, lemon juice, and sugar syrup. Process until a smooth purée forms, about 1 minute.

Pour the cantaloupe mixture into a 9-inch (23-cm) square metal pan or heavy dish. Freeze until the mixture is just frozen, about 1 hour. Using a fork, stir the granita to break up the ice crystals into clumps with a slushy texture. Return to the freezer and freeze until firm but not solid, up to 1 hour.

Spoon the granita into individual glasses or bowls and serve right away.

SERVES 2

CHOCOLATE POTS DE CRÈME

These delectable, silky smooth chocolate custards bake quickly and evenly in small ceramic ramekins. The individual portions are just right for serving two, whether it is a special occasion or you're both just craving chocolate.

INGREDIENTS

¼ cup (2 fl oz/ 60 ml) whole milk

6 Tbsp (3 fl oz/90 ml) heavy cream

1½ oz (45 g) best-quality bittersweet chocolate, finely chopped, plus more for optional garnish

2 large egg yolks

2½ Tbsp (1½ oz/45 g) sugar

Whipped cream for serving (optional)

TOOLS

serrated knife, mixing bowl and whisk or electric mixer (optional), saucepan, silicone spatula, wooden spoon, fine-mesh sieve, measuring pitcher, two ½-cup (4–fl oz/125-ml) ramekins or custard cups, deep baking dish, rasp grater (optional)

Preheat the oven to 300°F (150°C). In a saucepan over medium heat, combine the milk and cream and heat until small bubbles appear along the sides of the pan. Add the chocolate and stir with a silicone spatula just until the chocolate is melted. Set the mixture aside to cool slightly.

In a bowl, gently stir together the egg yolks and sugar with a wooden spoon until the sugar is dissolved. Slowly pour the warm (not hot) chocolate mixture into the egg yolk mixture while stirring constantly. Pour through a fine-mesh sieve into a measuring pitcher. Spoon off any foam from the surface.

Arrange two ½-cup (4–fl oz/125-ml) ramekins, custard cups, or other ovenproof dishes in a deep baking dish. Divide the chocolate mixture evenly between the ramekins. Pour hot water into the dish to reach about halfway up the sides of the ramekins. Cover the baking dish loosely with foil to prevent a skin from forming on the custards. Bake until the custards are just firm at the edges but still tremble in the center when the ramekins are shaken gently, about 30 minutes.

Remove the baking dish from the oven and carefully remove the ramekins from the water. Allow to cool completely before covering and refrigerating for at least 2 hours or up to overnight to set.

Serve the custards chilled. If desired, spoon a dollop of whipped cream on each custard and grate a dusting of chocolate over the top.

SERVES 2

4

DINNER *for* COMPANY

DINNER *for* COMPANY

At our house, simple, casual dinners for company are rarely that. We can't help ourselves. Sometimes it's like we're running a restaurant for our friends.

Jordan Every dinner party runs at least four courses: first, main, salad, and cheese. Often we add dessert and hors d'oeuvres, plus wine, of course.

Christie Our dinner parties follow a set pattern. Champagne to start and always a plate of noshes. I typically make a vegetarian soup or a salad for the first course. Here, we're on white wine, usually French. Then, the meat or fish comes out of the oven or off of the grill. We used to plate in the kitchen, though lately we've been serving family style. Now, the red wine flows. A refreshing *salade verte* comes next, followed by a cheese platter. Dessert is usually a vivid expression of whatever fruits are in season.

Jordan Our elaborate, multi-course meals reflect who we are. Christie has been in fine-dining service for most of her working life. That means that the house gets scrubbed, flowers appear, and wineglasses are polished. I take to the kitchen like I take to writing: every dish must have an original twist. I make my own stock for soups and start sauces a day in advance. At least I've stopped the sourdough-bread making!

Christie When the last guests have gone, you might think that we just collapse into bed. But sometimes that doesn't happen. Instead, if you're eavesdropping, you might hear the hiss of cold beer being uncapped and the blare of funky music being cranked up on the stereo. And then you'd see us sliding and spinning on the hardwood floors, dancing off the night's adrenaline.

QUICK IDEAS *for* SIMPLE GRAIN SIDES

Main courses at our house tend to be meticulously planned and executed. But when it comes to side dishes, we take a more casual approach. Occasionally we think them out in advance, but more often we buy whatever looks great at the market and go from there.

Great grain side dishes should be simple, yet flavorful enough to stand on their own. We start with our favorite grains—*farro*, quinoa, and couscous (actually a pasta)—as the base. Then we add copious amounts of fresh herbs and aromatics like garlic and shallots and finish them off with a splash of lemon juice or vinegar and a generous drizzle of fruity olive oil.

GREEN COUSCOUS
Purée 1 cup (1 oz/30 g) mixed fresh mint, basil, parsley, and sage leaves + drizzle of extra-virgin olive oil + salt and pepper; stir into 4 cups (1¼ lb/625 g) cooked couscous.

FARRO WITH BUTTERNUT SQUASH
Combine 4 cups (1½ lb/750 g) cooked *farro* + handful steamed diced butternut squash + 1 shallot, minced + 1 Tbsp melted butter + small handful chopped fresh thyme.

WILD RICE WITH CRANBERRIES
Combine 4 cups (1¼ lb/625 g) cooked wild rice + handful dried cranberries + 1 bunch green onions, chopped + drizzle each of sherry vinegar and extra-virgin olive oil + salt and pepper.

QUICK IDEAS *for* SIMPLE VEGETABLE SIDES

In fact, we often figure out the side dish while standing at the stove. We've found that interesting side dishes are often just a combination of two or three ingredients that you don't always find together; so we like to experiment. We also like to make the most of seasonal ingredients.

When it comes to creating healthful and tasty sides, one of our go-to dishes is what we call beans and greens, which is made by sautéing any variety of cooked beans with whatever hearty greens we have on hand, from Swiss chard to kale to beet greens, with red pepper flakes or grated cheese added for flavor. When we are preparing a main course that requires a lot of stove-top use, we roast vegetables to serve on the side. Roasting saves burner space, and the vegetables caramelize deliciously in the heat of the oven.

WHITE BEANS WITH TOMATOES
Sauté 2 Tbsp olive oil + handful chopped green onions + 1 tomato, diced + 1 can white beans, drained and rinsed; add splash chicken broth + salt and pepper + chopped fresh flat-leaf parsley.

CHANA MASALA
Sauté 2 Tbsp olive oil + 1 yellow onion, chopped + 1 can chickpeas, drained and rinsed + 1 can diced tomatoes + 2 Tbsp grated peeled fresh ginger + pinch each curry powder, ground cumin, and ground cinnamon + salt and pepper.

SAUTÉED GREEN BEANS
Sauté 1 Tbsp olive oil + 2 handfuls green beans + 2 cloves garlic, chopped + 1 red bell pepper, seeded and chopped; stir in handful chopped fresh cilantro + salt and pepper.

ROASTED CAULIFLOWER WITH CAPERS
Cut 2 heads cauliflower into florets and drizzle with olive oil; roast in a 450°F (230°C) oven for 30 minutes; toss with capers + grated zest and juice of 1 lemon.

ROASTED SWEET POTATOES WITH MAPLE GLAZE
Cut 3 sweet potatoes into wedges and toss with maple syrup + olive oil + dried rosemary + salt and pepper; roast in a 450°F (230°C) oven for 35 minutes.

SHAVED ZUCCHINI SALAD
WITH LEMON, MINT, AND FETA

Salty, tangy feta cheese and cool, refreshing mint brighten the naturally mild flavor of the zucchini in this simple salad. Use a top-notch extra-virgin olive oil to infuse the dish with rich, fruity flavor. If you use a vegetable peeler to cut the zucchini, make sure it is razor sharp. You want the strips paper thin and uniform.

INGREDIENTS

4 zucchini, about 2 lb (1 kg) total weight

¼ cup (2 fl oz/60 ml) extra-virgin olive oil

1 tsp finely grated lemon zest

Salt and freshly ground pepper

¼ cup (⅓ oz/10 g) torn fresh mint leaves

1 cup (5 oz/155 g) crumbled feta cheese

TOOLS

rasp grater, chef's knife, vegetable peeler or mandoline, assorted mixing bowls

Trim the ends of the zucchini but do not peel. Using a vegetable peeler or a mandoline, shave the zucchini lengthwise into long, paper-thin strips, letting the strips fall into a bowl. (Don't worry if you are unable to shave the seedy cores; discard them or reserve for another use.)

In a small bowl, whisk together the olive oil and lemon zest. Drizzle this mixture over the zucchini and season with ¼ teaspoon each salt and pepper. Add the mint and cheese to the bowl and toss gently. Taste and adjust the seasoning.

Transfer the salad to glasses or individual plates and serve.

SERVES 4–6

BABY GREENS SALAD WITH ROASTED STRAWBERRIES

Roasting strawberries with a bit of sugar intensifies their sweetness and softens their texture, creating a nice counterpoint to the salty cheese and crunchy almonds. You can top the salad with crumbled fresh goat cheese in place of the pecorino, if you like.

INGREDIENTS

2 pt (1 lb/500 g) large strawberries, hulled and cut in half lengthwise

8 Tbsp (4 fl oz/125 ml) extra-virgin olive oil

1 Tbsp plus 2 tsp sugar

Salt and freshly ground pepper

6 Tbsp (3 fl oz/90 ml) red wine vinegar

¼ cup (2 fl oz/60 ml) fresh orange juice

4 tsp finely chopped fresh tarragon leaves

1 cup (5½ oz/170 g) blanched whole almonds, toasted

9 cups (9 oz/280 g) baby spinach

5 oz (155 g) *pecorino romano* cheese, shaved

TOOLS

paring knife, chef's knife, citrus reamer or press, vegetable peeler, rimmed baking sheet, assorted mixing bowls, whisk

Preheat the oven to 400°F (200°C).

Spread the berries on a rimmed baking sheet. Drizzle with 2 tablespoons of the olive oil and sprinkle with the 2 teaspoons sugar, ¼ teaspoon salt, and several grinds of pepper. Toss to coat the berries evenly, then spread them out again. Roast until softened, about 10 minutes. Let cool to room temperature.

In a small bowl, whisk together the vinegar, orange juice, tarragon, the remaining 1 tablespoon sugar, ¾ teaspoon salt, and several grinds of pepper until the sugar dissolves. Slowly whisk in the remaining 6 tablespoons (3 fl oz/90 ml) olive oil until well blended to make a vinaigrette. Taste and adjust the seasoning.

In a small bowl, stir together the almonds and ¼ teaspoon salt. In a large bowl, combine the spinach, ¼ teaspoon salt, and several grinds of pepper. Whisk the vinaigrette to recombine, drizzle about one-half of it over the spinach, and toss well. Taste and adjust the seasoning and add more dressing if desired (you may not use all of it).

Divide the dressed spinach evenly among individual plates. Top each serving with some of the roasted strawberries, sprinkle with the almonds and cheese, and serve.

SERVES 6

ORANGE, ONION, AND OLIVE SALAD

Southern Mediterranean cooks like to combine sweet citrus with the tempered heat of red onion and the saltiness of olives. This delicious blend of flavors and textures offers a wonderful template for building other fruit salads. For example, use watermelon and lime juice instead of oranges and lemon juice, and add a scattering of crumbled feta cheese with the red onion and olives.

INGREDIENTS

4 navel oranges

¼ small red onion, thinly sliced

Juice of ½ lemon

¼ tsp ground cinnamon

1 Tbsp extra-virgin olive oil

Salt and freshly ground pepper

½ cup (3 oz/90 g) Castelvetrano green olives or salt-cured black olives, pitted and halved

1 Tbsp chopped fresh flat-leaf parsley

TOOLS

chef's knife, citrus reamer or press, paring knife, small mixing bowl, whisk

Working with 1 orange at a time, and using a sharp knife, cut a slice off both ends of the orange to reveal the flesh. Stand the orange upright on a cutting board and, using the knife, cut downward to remove the peel and pith in thick strips, following the contour of the fruit. Cut the orange crosswise into slices ½ inch (12 mm) thick. Pour any orange juice from the cutting board into a small bowl. Repeat with the remaining oranges.

Arrange the orange slices on a serving platter, overlapping them slightly to cover the plate nicely. Scatter the onion slices over the top.

Add the lemon juice and cinnamon to the reserved orange juice and whisk until blended. Whisk in the olive oil to make a dressing. Season to taste with salt and pepper.

Scatter the olives over the oranges and drizzle with the dressing. Let sit at room temperature for 10–15 minutes to allow the flavors to blend. Sprinkle with the parsley and serve.

SERVES 4

SIMPLE FISH BOUILLABAISSE

Here is an easy version of the famed fish soup of Marseilles, crowned with fennel fronds, chervil, and orange zest and accompanied with crunchy crostini. We recommend pouring a rosé (see note), but you can also open a good-quality dry white for cooking and enjoy the rest at the dinner table.

INGREDIENTS

2 Tbsp extra-virgin olive oil

10 cloves garlic, thinly sliced

1 Tbsp fennel seeds

3 bay leaves

¼ cup (2 oz/60 g) tomato paste

Salt and freshly ground pepper

⅓ cup (3 fl oz/80 ml) dry white wine

1 large fennel bulb

1 can (15 oz/470 g) crushed tomatoes, with juice

5 cups (40 fl oz/1.25 l) fish or vegetable broth

2 lb (1 kg) cod or monkfish fillets, cut into 2-inch (5-cm) chunks

Shredded zest of 1 orange

2 Tbsp chopped fresh chervil (optional)

Crostini (page 92) for serving

TOOLS

chef's knife, citrus grater, large Dutch oven, slotted spoon, immersion blender or blender, ladle

DRINK NOTE

Matching bouillabaisse with wine can be perplexing. The presence of fish points toward white wine, but the added weight of tomato broth suggests red. Our solution? Meet the choices halfway with a dry rosé, preferably one from Provence, where this soup originates.

In a large Dutch oven over low heat, warm the olive oil. Add the garlic, fennel seeds, and bay leaves and cook gently, stirring occasionally, until the garlic is fragrant and tender, about 10 minutes. Do not let the garlic brown. Stir in the tomato paste and 1½ teaspoons salt and cook, stirring, for 2 minutes. Pour in the wine and stir to combine.

Cut off the stems and feathery fronds of the fennel bulb and remove any bruised or discolored outer layers. Coarsely chop the feathery tops to yield 2 tablespoons and set aside. Cut the bulb lengthwise into wedges and trim away the core, leaving a little core intact to hold each wedge together. Add the fennel wedges, tomatoes with their juice, and broth to the Dutch oven, cover, and cook at a gentle simmer for 1 hour. Add the fish, re-cover, and cook for 10–15 minutes more. The fish should be firm but tender.

Using a slotted spoon, transfer the fish and fennel wedges to a plate. Purée the soup with an immersion blender. (Alternatively, for a chunkier soup, transfer half of the mixture to a blender, process until smooth, then return to the Dutch oven and stir to combine.)

Ladle the tomato broth into shallow bowls and divide the fish and fennel wedges evenly among the bowls. Garnish each serving with a little orange zest, the reserved chopped fennel tops, and the chervil, if using. Season with pepper and serve with the crostini.

SERVES 4–6

SMOKY BEEF CHILI

To add color and flavor to this slow-simmered chili, top each serving with some corn salsa: In a bowl, toss together 2 cups (12 oz/375 g) each fresh or thawed frozen corn kernels and halved cherry tomatoes; 4 green onions, including the tender green tops, thinly sliced; and the juice of 1 lime.

INGREDIENTS

4 lb (2 kg) boneless beef chuck, trimmed of most fat and cut into ¾-inch (2-cm) cubes

Salt and freshly ground pepper

¼ cup (2 fl oz/60 ml) canola oil

2 large yellow onions, coarsely chopped

8 cloves garlic, sliced

2 chipotle chiles in adobo sauce, finely chopped

2 Tbsp chipotle chile powder

2 tsp ground cumin

1 tsp dried oregano, preferably Mexican

½–1 tsp red pepper flakes

1 cup (8 oz/250 g) tomato paste

2–3 cups (16–24 fl oz/ 500–750 ml) beef broth

TOOLS

chef's knife, Dutch oven, slotted spoon, wooden spoon, ladle

Season the beef generously with salt and pepper. In a Dutch oven over high heat, warm the oil. When the oil is hot, working in batches to avoid crowding, add the beef and sear, turning as needed to brown evenly, until golden brown on all sides, about 5 minutes total. Using a slotted spoon, transfer the beef to a plate.

Pour off most of the fat from the pan and return to medium heat. Add the onions and sauté until softened, about 6 minutes. Add the garlic and cook for 1 minute longer. Add the chipotle chiles and sauce, chile powder, cumin, oregano, red pepper flakes to taste, and the tomato paste, stir well, and cook for 2 minutes. Pour in 1 cup (8 fl oz/250 ml) of the broth and stir with a wooden spoon to dislodge any browned bits from the pan bottom. Add ½ teaspoon salt, a few grinds of pepper, and 1 cup broth if you prefer a thicker, more intensely flavored chili, or 2 cups broth if you prefer a soupier chili (for spooning over rice or moistening corn bread). Stir in the browned beef. Reduce the heat to low so that the chili is barely simmering, cover, and cook until the meat is very tender, about 1½ hours.

Ladle the chili into bowls and serve.

SERVES 8

THREE-CHEESE LASAGNE

Yes, lasagne is time-consuming to make. But when it is done well, nothing can beat it. We plan ahead and do a couple of steps each day. For example, we make the tomato sauce way in advance and refrigerate or freeze it until ready to use. We also make the ricotta mixture a day ahead of time. And finally, once we put the whole thing together, it can sit for a couple of days in the fridge before we bake it.

INGREDIENTS

Extra-virgin olive oil for drizzling

4 cups (2 lb/1 kg) ricotta cheese

½ cup (2 oz/60 g) freshly grated Parmesan cheese

1 lb (500 g) fresh mozzarella cheese, cubed

2 cloves garlic, minced

1 Tbsp chopped fresh flat-leaf parsley

Salt and freshly ground pepper

2 large eggs, lightly beaten

3 cups (24 fl oz/750 ml) Tomato-Basil Sauce (page 250) or purchased tomato sauce

½ lb (250 g) fresh pasta sheets (page 250) or no-boil dried lasagne noodles

TOOLS

rasp grater, chef's knife, assorted mixing bowls, 9-inch (23-cm) square pan, wooden spoon, ladle, silicone spatula

Preheat the oven to 375°F (190°C). Lightly drizzle olive oil evenly over the bottom of a 9-inch (23-cm) square pan with 3-inch (7.5-cm) sides.

In a large bowl, stir together the ricotta, Parmesan, and all but 1 cup (4 oz/125 g) of the mozzarella. Add the garlic, parsley, 1 teaspoon salt, and a few grinds of pepper. Taste and adjust with more salt if needed. Add the eggs and mix well.

Ladle ½ cup (4 fl oz/125 ml) of the tomato sauce onto the bottom of the prepared pan, spread to cover evenly, and arrange 1 layer of pasta, trimmed or broken to fit as needed, on top of the sauce. Spread one-third of the cheese mixture evenly over the pasta. Top with a layer of pasta, ladle ¾ cup (6 fl oz/180 ml) of the sauce over the pasta, and then top with another layer of pasta. Repeat the layering: cheese mixture, pasta, sauce, pasta, cheese mixture, pasta, and finally the remaining 1 cup (8 fl oz/250 ml) sauce, spreading it evenly. Sprinkle the reserved mozzarella over the top. (At this point, the lasagne can be tightly covered and refrigerated for up to 2 days or frozen for up to 2 months.)

Bake until the cheese is golden and bubbling and the noodles are tender, 40–45 minutes. (If baking frozen or refrigerated lasagne, cover with aluminum foil for the first 30 minutes, uncover, and bake for 30–45 minutes longer.) Let rest for 10 minutes before serving.

SERVES 4–6

GRILLED FISH TACOS

Tacos are infinitely customizable and you get to eat them with your hands—what could be better? Lots of lime is imperative. Instead of using lettuce, we often like to make our tacos Baja style, which calls for a quickly made slaw of cabbage, lime juice, cilantro, chile powder, and a dab of mayo.

INGREDIENTS

1 Tbsp canola oil, plus more for grill grate and for brushing

2 jalapeño chiles, quartered lengthwise and seeded

6 skinless snapper or other firm white fish fillets, each 4–5 oz (125–155 g)

Salt and freshly ground pepper

4–8 corn tortillas, 6 inches (15 cm) in diameter

1 handful hardwood chips, soaked in water for 30 minutes

½ head iceberg lettuce, shredded

1½ cups (9 oz/280 g) fresh tomato salsa

Fresh cilantro, chopped white or yellow onions, tomatoes, and cucumbers for serving (optional)

Hot-pepper sauce and lime wedges for serving

TOOLS

paring knife, chef's knife, charcoal or gas grill, small mixing bowl, pastry brush, wide spatula, carving board

Prepare a charcoal or gas grill for direct grilling over medium-high heat and oil the grill grate.

In a small bowl, toss the chiles with the 1 tablespoon canola oil. Brush the fish with oil, season with salt and pepper, and set aside. Working in batches, grill the tortillas until warmed, 1–2 minutes. Wrap in foil or a kitchen towel to keep warm.

If using a charcoal grill, sprinkle the wood chips over the coals. Place the chiles over the hottest part of the fire. Grill, turning once, until nicely charred, 1–2 minutes per side. Grill the fish over the hottest part of the fire until opaque and nicely charred, 3–5 minutes. Using a wide spatula, carefully turn the fish and grill until cooked through, 3–4 minutes longer.

If using a gas grill, raise a burner to high heat. Heat a smoker box half full of wood chips until smoking; reduce the heat to medium-low. Place the chiles over the heating elements. Grill, turning once, until nicely charred, 1–2 minutes per side. Grill the fish over the heating elements until opaque and nicely charred, 3–5 minutes. Using a wide spatula, carefully turn the fish and grill until cooked through, 3–4 minutes longer.

Transfer the fish to a carving board and flake each fillet into large pieces. To assemble the tacos, arrange pieces of fish on each tortilla. Top with the grilled chiles, lettuce, salsa, cilantro, and other toppings of your choice. Serve with hot-pepper sauce and lime wedges.

SERVES 4

CHICKEN TAGINE WITH OLIVES AND LEMONS

This rustic, hearty dish, flavored with preserved lemons and green olives, is an adaptation of a classic Moroccan *tagine*, or stew. Look for the salt-cured lemons in a Middle Eastern grocery, a specialty-foods store, or online.

INGREDIENTS

¼ tsp saffron threads

2 large yellow onions, about 1 lb (500 g) total weight, diced

½ cup (¾ oz/20 g) coarsely chopped fresh cilantro

½ cup (¾ oz/20 g) coarsely chopped fresh flat-leaf parsley

4 Tbsp (2 fl oz/60 ml) fresh lemon juice

1 tsp ground cumin

½ tsp ground ginger

½ tsp ground turmeric

Salt

2 large cloves garlic, crushed

3 Tbsp extra-virgin olive oil

8 skinless, bone-in chicken thighs

1 skinless, bone-in whole chicken breast, about 1¼ lb (625 g), cut into 4 pieces

2 preserved lemons

½ cup (4 fl oz/125 ml) chicken broth

1½ cups (8 oz/250 g) green olives, cracked with the side of a large chef's knife

TOOLS

chef's knife, citrus reamer or press, small mixing bowl, food processor, large Dutch oven, saucepan, colander

In a small bowl, combine the saffron with 2 tablespoons warm water and set aside to soak for 10 minutes.

In a food processor, combine the onions, cilantro, parsley, 2 tablespoons of the lemon juice, the cumin, ginger, turmeric, saffron and its soaking liquid, and 1 teaspoon salt and process to a pulpy purée. Transfer to a large resealable plastic bag and add the garlic and olive oil. Add the chicken pieces to the marinade, seal the bag, and massage to coat the chicken with the mixture. Refrigerate for at least 8 hours or up to 24 hours.

Halve the preserved lemons and scoop out the pulp onto the cutting board. Cut the rind of both lemons into strips ¼ inch (6 mm) wide and set aside. Chop half of the pulp and set aside. Discard the remaining pulp.

Transfer the chicken with the marinade to a large Dutch oven. Pour in the broth, add the lemon pulp, and bring to a boil over medium-high heat. Cover, reduce the heat to medium-low, and simmer until the chicken is tender when pierced with a sharp knife, about 40 minutes. Meanwhile, bring a saucepan filled with water to a boil, add the olives, adjust the heat, and simmer for 5 minutes. Drain and set aside.

When the chicken is tender, add the olives, the lemon-rind strips, and the remaining 2 tablespoons lemon juice to the pot. Re-cover and simmer until the chicken is falling-off-the-bone tender, 10–15 minutes longer.

Serve directly from the pot or transfer the contents to a wide, shallow serving bowl.

SERVES 6–8

PENNE ALL'ARRABBIATA

This lightly sauced Roman-style pasta takes its name, which means "angry pasta," from the fiery bite of the red pepper flakes. For a casual dinner with friends, accompany the pasta with a green salad and some crusty bread and follow with a simple dessert of fresh fruit, gelato, or affogato, a scoop of vanilla gelato topped with a shot of hot espresso.

INGREDIENTS

2 Tbsp extra-virgin olive oil

3 oz (90 g) pancetta, diced

1 yellow onion, finely chopped

2 cloves garlic, minced

¾–1 tsp red pepper flakes

1 can (28 oz/875 g) whole plum tomatoes

Salt

1 lb (500 g) penne

½ cup (2 oz/60 g) freshly grated *pecorino romano* cheese

¼ cup (⅓ oz/10 g) chopped fresh flat-leaf parsley

TOOLS

chef's knife, rasp grater, large frying pan, large pot, colander

In a large frying pan over medium heat, warm the olive oil. Add the pancetta and cook, stirring often, until browned, 2–3 minutes. Add the onion, garlic, and red pepper flakes to taste and sauté until the onion is soft and translucent, 3–5 minutes. Stir in the tomatoes with their juice and ½ teaspoon salt, using a fork to crush and break up the tomatoes. Simmer, uncovered, until the sauce has thickened slightly, 10–15 minutes. Remove from the heat and keep warm.

Meanwhile, bring a large pot of salted water to a boil. Add the penne, stir, and cook, stirring occasionally, until al dente, according to the package directions. Drain the pasta.

Transfer the drained pasta to the pan with the sauce, place over low heat, and toss briefly to coat thoroughly. Add half of the cheese and toss to mix evenly. Transfer to a warmed serving bowl, sprinkle with the parsley, and serve. Pass the remaining cheese at the table.

SERVES 4–6

OLIVE OIL-BRAISED TUNA WITH TAPENADE

Tuna, which is lean and dries out easily, is often seared quickly over high heat and served rare. But here, we cook it gently over low heat with a little broth, which yields moist, flavorful flesh. The result pairs well with bold flavors, such as our garlic-laden, citrusy tapenade.

INGREDIENTS

¼ cup (2 fl oz/60 ml) fish or vegetable broth

5 Tbsp (3 fl oz/80 ml) extra-virgin olive oil, plus more for drizzling

¼ cup (2 fl oz/60 ml) dry white wine or rosé

½ yellow onion, finely chopped

3 bay leaves

Salt and freshly ground pepper

1½ lb (750 g) skinless tuna fillets or steaks, cut into 4 equal pieces

1 cup (5 oz/155 g) pitted mild green olives such as Picholine or Lucques

1 cup (5 oz/155 g) pitted black olives such as Niçoise or Kalamata

2 cloves garlic, chopped

1 tsp red or white wine vinegar

Grated zest of 1 orange

4 cups (4 oz/125 g) baby spinach

TOOLS

paring knife, chef's knife, sauté pan with lid, rasp grater, food processor, mixing bowl

In a sauté pan, stir together the broth, 4 tablespoons (2 fl oz/60 ml) of the olive oil, the wine, onion, bay leaves, ½ teaspoon salt, and several grinds of pepper. Cover and cook on low heat for 30 minutes to blend the flavors. Add the tuna, re-cover, and cook for 15–20 minutes longer. The tuna should be firm and opaque throughout.

In a food processor, combine the green and black olives, the garlic, the remaining 1 tablespoon olive oil, the vinegar, and the orange zest. Pulse to form a chunky tapenade. (You will not need all of the tapenade for this dish. Store the remainder in an airtight container in the refrigerator for up to 1 week. Use it on broiled or grilled fish, in sandwiches, or as a dip.)

In a bowl, drizzle the spinach with a little olive oil, season with salt and pepper, and toss to coat evenly. Divide the spinach among individual plates, and then divide the tuna among the plates, arranging it on top of the spinach. Top each tuna portion with a spoonful of the tapenade and serve.

SERVES 4

real couple stories

WHAT IS YOUR APPROACH TO ENTERTAINING?

Molly and Brandon

As with our cooking, we keep it simple, casual, and off the cuff. We like the kind of nights when everyone hangs out in the kitchen, leaning against the counter with a drink in hand. Food-wise, we usually make either pasta—easy and satisfying—or something you can eat with your hands, like a big pile of local crab or prawns. Eating that way puts everyone at ease.

Aki and Alex

Relaxed. We want to be able to enjoy our guests and the process of feeding them a good meal. We often play country music while cooking because it keeps us moving in the kitchen.

Saukok and Jamie

Great food is key, but equally important is having time to enjoy being with our guests. We plan things out and prep most items before guests arrive, and clean as we go along. A barbecue on our rooftop is our idea of a perfect dinner party. On the menu: baby back pork ribs, corn on the cob, and zucchini marinated with homemade vinegar.

Julie and Matt

We like to involve everyone in preparing the food. Part of enjoying a meal is working with the pieces that bring the feast together. We set our table with vintage tableware and cloth napkins.

Lisa and Emmett

Casual. We like to move the party from the kitchen (hanging around the center island as we cook or make cocktails) to the dining room table to the outdoor table to the patio. We always have lots of candles and good music. For starters, we often serve tapas-style food: spiced nuts, marinated cheeses, skewers, grilled breads with toppings.

GRILLED CHICKEN WITH CORN
AND SMOKED MOZZARELLA SALAD

When it's too hot to turn on the oven, we fire up the grill for this summertime meal of roasted whole chicken. Smoked mozzarella has a firm, creamy texture that pairs well with the corn and tomatoes in the chunky, colorful salad.

INGREDIENTS

1 whole chicken, about 4 lb (2 kg)

¼ cup (2 fl oz/60 ml) plus 1 Tbsp extra-virgin olive oil

Salt and freshly ground pepper

Canola oil for brushing and for grill grate

2 ears corn

1 Tbsp white or regular balsamic vinegar

1 clove garlic, minced

½ lb (250 g) smoked mozzarella cheese, cut into ½-inch (12-mm) cubes

1 cup (6 oz/185 g) cherry tomatoes, halved

3 Tbsp coarsely torn fresh basil leaves

TOOLS

chef's knife, pastry brush, charcoal or gas grill, instant-read thermometer, whisk, carving board

Pull off the fat from around the chicken's cavity and discard. Brush the chicken all over with the 1 tablespoon olive oil and season inside and out with salt and pepper. Let the chicken stand at room temperature while you prepare the grill and corn.

Prepare a charcoal or gas grill for indirect cooking over high heat and oil the grill grate. Remove the husks and silk from the corn and wrap each ear in foil.

Place the chicken, breast side up, on the cool side of the grill. Place the foil-wrapped corn on the hot side of the grill. Cover the grill and cook the corn, turning occasionally, until the kernels are lightly toasted (open the foil to check), about 15 minutes. Transfer the corn to a plate, unwrap the ears, and let cool. Continue to cook the chicken, covered, until an instant-read thermometer inserted into the thickest part of the breast away from the bone registers 165°F (75°C), about 50 minutes longer.

Meanwhile, when the corn is cool enough to handle, use a chef's knife to cut the ears in half crosswise. One at a time, stand the halves, flat end down, on a work surface and cut the kernels from the cob.

In a serving bowl, whisk together the vinegar, garlic, ½ teaspoon salt, and ¼ teaspoon pepper. Gradually whisk in the ¼ cup olive oil. Add the corn, cheese, cherry tomatoes, and basil and mix gently. Taste and adjust the seasoning. Set aside at room temperature to allow the flavors to blend while the chicken finishes cooking.

When the chicken is ready, transfer to a carving board and let rest for 10 minutes. Carve the chicken and serve with the salad.

SERVES 4

ROASTED CHICKEN WITH
WARM WINTER GREENS SALAD

Coating a chicken with its own rendered fat will yield a golden bird with appealingly crisp skin, but you can skip this step and substitute olive oil if you're short on time. We like to transform the pan drippings into a robust vinaigrette for a seasonal salad of sturdy greens.

INGREDIENTS

1 whole chicken, about 4 lb (2 kg)

2 slices coarse country bread, each ¾ inch (2 cm) thick, cut into cubes

2 Tbsp extra-virgin olive oil

Salt and freshly ground pepper

1 shallot, minced

1 clove garlic, minced

½ cup (4 fl oz/125 ml) chicken broth

2 Tbsp sherry vinegar

2 Tbsp walnut oil

6–8 cups (4–5 oz/ 125–155 g) mixed winter salad greens such as frisée, radicchio, escarole, and chicory

½ cup (2 oz/60 g) walnuts, toasted and coarsely chopped

½ cup (2 oz/60 g) dried cranberries

TOOLS

serrated bread knife, chef's knife, small saucepan, fine-mesh sieve, assorted mixing bowls, rimmed baking sheet, V-shaped roasting rack, roasting pan, instant-read thermometer, carving board, wooden spoon

DRINK NOTE

Whites and light reds such as Pinot Noir will always complement roasted chicken. But this robust, crispy chicken can stand up to an earthier, juicier red such as a Syrah from the northern Rhône. Look for appellations like Saint-Joseph, Cornas, and Crozes-Hermitage.

Pull off the fat from around the chicken's cavity and chop coarsely. In a small saucepan over low heat, cook the fat until rendered, about 15 minutes. Strain through a fine-mesh sieve; you should have about 1½ tablespoons. Let the chicken and fat stand at cool room temperature for 1–2 hours.

Preheat the oven to 350°F (180°C). Put the bread cubes in a bowl, drizzle with the olive oil, toss, and spread on a rimmed baking sheet. Toast in the oven, stirring occasionally, until golden, about 15 minutes. Let cool.

Raise the oven temperature to 425°F (220°C). Place a V-shaped rack in a roasting pan. Rub the rendered fat all over the chicken and season the chicken inside and out with salt and pepper. Place the chicken on its side on the rack and roast for 20 minutes. Turn the chicken on its other side and roast for 20 minutes longer. Turn it on its back and roast until golden brown and an instant-read thermometer inserted into the thickest part of the breast away from the bone registers 165°F (75°C), about 40 minutes.

Tilt the bird so any juice in the cavity flows into the pan, then transfer to a carving board and let rest for 10 minutes. Pour off all but 2 tablespoons of the drippings from the pan. Place the pan on the stove top over medium heat. Add the shallot and garlic and cook, stirring, until soft, about 2 minutes. Stir in the broth, vinegar, and walnut oil to make a vinaigrette, and bring to a boil over high heat, scraping up any browned bits with a wooden spoon. Remove from the heat. Taste and adjust the seasoning.

In a large bowl, combine the salad greens, bread cubes, walnuts, and cranberries. Add the vinaigrette and toss to coat. Divide the salad among individual plates. Cut the chicken into quarters, place one on each salad, and serve.

SERVES 4

GRILLED STEAK WITH CHIMICHURRI

In Argentina, where grilled meats are popular, *salsa chimichurri* is a ubiquitous condiment. Although its bright acidity and bracing garlic and herbal flavors are traditionally enjoyed with meats, the sauce also complements chicken, fish, and even vegetables.

INGREDIENTS

FOR THE CHIMICHURRI

1 cup (1 oz/30 g) fresh flat-leaf parsley leaves

1 cup (1 oz/30 g) fresh cilantro leaves

3 Tbsp fresh marjoram leaves

4 cloves garlic

Salt and freshly ground black pepper

3 Tbsp Champagne vinegar

½ cup (4 fl oz/125 ml) extra-virgin olive oil

½ red bell pepper, roasted, peeled, seeded, and finely diced

1 Tbsp red pepper flakes (optional)

3 sirloin strip steaks, each about ½ lb (250 g) and 1 inch (2.5 cm) thick

Salt and freshly ground black pepper

Extra-virgin olive oil for brushing

TOOLS

chef's knife, food processor, silicone spatula, pastry brush, charcoal or gas grill or stove-top grill pan, tongs, carving board

DRINK NOTE

One reason we like to grill steaks is because it gives us the best excuse for drinking the big reds we love. That means uncorking a Cabernet Sauvignon from any of the many places in which it is made. But the pungent, piquant *chimichurri* suggests a wine with spice, too, making an Argentine Malbec another great choice.

To make the *chimichurri*, in a food processor, combine the parsley, cilantro, marjoram, and garlic and pulse several times to chop coarsely. Scrape down the sides of the bowl and season the sauce generously with salt and black pepper. Add the vinegar and pulse to incorporate. With the machine running, add the olive oil in a slow, steady stream until emulsified. Pour into a small serving bowl. Stir in the roasted bell pepper and the red pepper flakes, if using. Cover tightly and let stand while you prepare the steaks, or refrigerate up to overnight. Remove from the refrigerator 20 minutes before grilling.

Trim off the excess fat from the steaks; reserve a 1-inch (2.5-cm) piece to grease the grill grate. Generously season the steaks with salt and black pepper and brush with olive oil.

Prepare a charcoal or gas grill for direct grilling over high heat. Using tongs, grease the preheated grill grate with the reserved fat; it should smoke and sizzle immediately and begin to melt. Place the steaks over the hottest part of the fire and grill, turning once, until nicely charred and cooked to your liking, 4–6 minutes per side for medium-rare.

Transfer the meat to a carving board, tent with foil, and let rest for 5 minutes. Slice the steaks across the grain and arrange on a platter. Pour any accumulated juices from the carving board over the top. Drizzle some of the *chimichurri* over the slices and serve. Pass the remaining *chimichurri* at the table.

SERVES 6

SEARED FIVE-SPICE DUCK BREASTS
WITH RHUBARB COMPOTE

Here, we use Chinese five-spice powder, a blend of warm, fragrant spices, to give meaty duck breasts an exotic, intriguing flavor. Look for firm, rose-colored rhubarb stalks at the market in spring and early summer. Remove any leaves and trim the stalks carefully of any strings before cutting them into pieces.

INGREDIENTS

4 boneless duck breast halves, about 7 oz (220 g) each

1 tsp Chinese five-spice powder

Salt and freshly ground pepper

1 large orange

4 or 5 rhubarb stalks, about 10 oz (315 g) total weight, cut into ½-inch (12-mm) pieces

½ cup (3½ oz/105 g) firmly packed light brown sugar

3-inch (7.5-cm) piece cinnamon stick

Ice cubes

TOOLS

chef's knife, assorted mixing bowls, rasp grater, citrus reamer or press, saucepan, slotted spoon, large frying pan, carving board

DRINK NOTE

Duck is red wine's best friend because almost every red is a good match. Pinot Noir from anywhere; Grenache from the United States, Australia, or France's southern Rhône; Sangiovese from central Italy; Nebbiolo from northern Italy; or Tempranillo from Spain— all of them are good with this dish.

Using a sharp chef's knife, score the skin of each duck breast half in a crosshatch pattern. In a small bowl, stir together the five-spice powder, 1 teaspoon salt, and ½ teaspoon pepper. Season the duck breasts on both sides with the mixture and let stand at room temperature for 30 minutes.

Finely grate the zest from the orange, then squeeze ½ cup (4 fl oz/125 ml) orange juice, supplementing with water if needed. In a saucepan over medium heat, combine the orange zest and juice, rhubarb, brown sugar, and cinnamon and bring to a boil, stirring often. Reduce the heat to medium-low and simmer, stirring occasionally, until the rhubarb is just tender, about 8 minutes.

Meanwhile, fill a large bowl with ice water. When the rhubarb is ready, using a slotted spoon, transfer the pieces to a heatproof bowl and nestle the bowl in the ice water. Return the juices in the pan to the stove, raise the heat to high, and boil the juices until syrupy, about 5 minutes. Pour the juices over the rhubarb, discard the cinnamon, and stir gently. Let cool.

Place the duck breasts, skin side down, in a large frying pan and place over medium-high heat. Cook until the skin is golden brown and has rendered its fat, about 7 minutes. Transfer the duck to a plate and pour off most of the fat from the pan. Return the duck breasts, skin side up, to the pan and place over medium-high heat. Cook until the undersides are nicely browned, about 7 minutes longer for medium-rare or until cooked to your liking.

Transfer the duck to a carving board and let rest for 5 minutes. Cut each breast across the grain into thin slices and transfer to individual plates. Spoon the compote alongside the duck and serve, passing the remaining compote at the table.

SERVES 4

HERB-ROASTED PORK LOIN

Serve this simple Tuscan-inspired pork dish with the roasted rosemary potatoes on page 184 and a good Italian red, preferably from Tuscany, such as a Chianti Classico or, if you feel like splurging, a Brunello di Montalcino.

INGREDIENTS

3 large cloves garlic, finely chopped

1½ Tbsp fresh rosemary leaves, finely chopped

1½ Tbsp fresh sage leaves, finely chopped

1½ tsp crushed fennel seeds

Salt and freshly ground pepper

1 bone-in pork loin roast, 3½–4 lb (1.75–2 kg)

3 Tbsp extra-virgin olive oil

1 small yellow onion, halved and sliced

¾ cup (6 fl oz/180 ml) dry white wine such as Pinot Grigio or dry vermouth

TOOLS

chef's knife, small mixing bowl, paring knife, roasting pan, instant-read thermometer, wooden spoon, carving board

Preheat the oven to 325°F (165°C).

In a small bowl, combine the garlic, rosemary, sage, and fennel seeds, season with salt and pepper, and mix well. With a paring knife, make slits ½ inch (12 mm) deep all over the pork roast and insert some of the mixture into each slit. Rub the roast with the remaining seasoning, then rub with 1½ tablespoons of the olive oil. Place the meat in a roasting pan just large enough to hold it.

Roast the meat for 45 minutes. In a bowl, toss the onion slices with the remaining 1½ tablespoons olive oil and scatter them around the meat. Continue to roast until an instant-read thermometer inserted into the thickest part of the roast away from bone registers 140°F (60°C), or the meat is pale pink at the center when cut into, about 50 minutes longer. Transfer to a platter, tent with foil, and let rest for 15 minutes before carving.

Meanwhile, pour off most of the fat in the roasting pan and place the pan over medium-low heat. Add the wine and deglaze the pan, stirring with a wooden spoon to scrape up any browned bits from the pan bottom. Simmer until the sauce is slightly reduced.

Carve the roast and arrange on a platter. Spoon the pan sauce over the pork and serve.

SERVES 6

PAELLA

Serve this colorful Spanish dish family style for a casual get-together, either spooned onto a platter or directly from the pan. If the mussels at your fish market look good, use them in place of or in addition to the clams, being careful to remove their beards before they go into the pan.

INGREDIENTS

2 Tbsp extra-virgin olive oil

1 lb (500 g) Spanish dry-cured chorizo, cut into slices ½ inch (12 mm) thick

1 yellow onion, chopped

1 red bell pepper, seeded and chopped

3 cloves garlic, minced

Salt and freshly ground pepper

2 cups (14 oz/440 g) long-grain white rice such as basmati

½ tsp saffron threads (optional)

4 cups (32 fl oz/1 l) chicken broth

1–2 lb (500 g–1 kg) small clams such as littleneck or Manila, scrubbed

1 lb (500 g) large shrimp, peeled and deveined

1 cup (5 oz/155 g) frozen baby peas

Lemon wedges for serving

TOOLS

chef's knife, paring knife, large frying pan or paella pan

DRINK NOTE

Even though this dish is loaded with seafood, it calls for red wine. That's because its saffron-tinged, dark-roasted flavors make it perfect for the deep berry, toasty character of Spanish Rioja, Ribera del Duero, or Toro. Lighter reds also work, like peppery Beaujolais or Côtes du Rhône.

In a large frying pan or paella pan over medium-high heat, warm the oil. Add the chorizo and cook, turning occasionally, until browned on both sides, about 3 minutes. Add the onion, bell pepper, and garlic and sauté until softened, 3–4 minutes. Season with salt and pepper. Add the rice, crumble in the saffron (if using), and cook, stirring, until the rice grains are well coated, about 2 minutes. Pour in the broth and stir in 1½ teaspoons salt. Bring to a boil, reduce the heat to low, cover, and cook until the rice has absorbed nearly all of the liquid, about 20 minutes.

Press the clams, hinge side down, into the rice, discarding any that do not close to the touch. Spread the shrimp over the rice and top with the peas. Cover and cook until the shrimp are opaque and the clams have opened, about 5 minutes longer. Discard any unopened clams and serve. Pass the lemon wedges at the table.

SERVES 4–6

STEAK AU POIVRE

For a lighter dish, omit the Cognac, cream, and tarragon. Add ½ pound (250 g) cremini mushrooms, thinly sliced, to the pan with the shallots and sauté until tender, about 5 minutes. Season with salt and freshly ground pepper and serve over the steak.

INGREDIENTS

1 Tbsp peppercorns

1 Tbsp coarse sea salt

4 rib-eye or New York strip steaks, each about 6 oz (185 g) and 1 inch (2.5 cm) thick

3 Tbsp unsalted butter

1 Tbsp canola oil

2 shallots, thinly sliced

⅓ cup (3 fl oz/80 ml) Cognac or brandy

⅓ cup (3 fl oz/80 ml) heavy cream

1 tsp chopped fresh tarragon (optional)

Salt and freshly ground pepper

TOOLS

chef's knife, rolling pin, small mixing bowl, 1 large frying pan or 2 medium frying pans, wooden spoon

DRINK NOTE

This French bistro classic is perfect with medium- to full-bodied, moderately fruity reds that have a hint of pepper to match the meat. Pick up a Cabernet-based Bordeaux (it doesn't have to be expensive), a Cabernet Franc from the Loire Valley, or your favorite Cabernet from Chile, California, Western Australia, or Washington.

Place the peppercorns in a small, heavy-duty resealable plastic bag. Coarsely crush them with a rolling pin. In a small bowl, stir together the crushed peppercorns and the coarse salt. Pat the mixture firmly and evenly onto both sides of the steaks.

In a large frying pan (or 2 medium pans) over medium-high heat, melt 2 tablespoons of the butter with the canola oil. Add the steaks and cook, turning once, until done to your liking, 6–8 minutes total for medium-rare. Transfer the steaks to a platter and tent with foil.

Add the remaining 1 tablespoon butter to the pan and place over medium heat. Add the shallots and sauté until soft, about 2 minutes. Stir in the Cognac, cream, and the tarragon, if using, and bring just to a boil, stirring with a wooden spoon to scrape up any browned bits on the pan bottom. Reduce the heat and simmer until slightly thickened, about 1 minute. Season to taste with salt and pepper. Divide the steaks among individual plates, spoon the sauce over them, and serve.

SERVES 4

MEDITERRANEAN LAMB SHANKS
WITH POMEGRANATE AND MINT

Once you have browned the shanks and sautéed the aromatics, this dish cooks slowly in the oven until the meat is almost falling off the bones, giving you plenty of time to prepare other dishes or to put your feet up and read a novel. Serve with a couscous and herb salad (see page 152) for a satisfying and easy cold-weather supper for company.

INGREDIENTS

4–6 lamb shanks, about 1 lb (500 g) each, trimmed of most of their fat

Salt and freshly ground pepper

2 Tbsp extra-virgin olive oil

1 large yellow onion, finely chopped

2 cinnamon sticks

6 whole cloves

10 allspice berries

¼ cup (2 fl oz/60 ml) brandy

1 can (15 oz/470 g) diced tomatoes, drained

½ cup (4 fl oz/125 ml) beef broth

2 Tbsp coarsely chopped fresh mint

¼ cup (1 oz/30 g) pomegranate seeds

TOOLS

chef's knife, colander, large Dutch oven, tongs, wooden spoon, fine-mesh sieve, small saucepan

Preheat the oven to 325°F (165°C). Season the lamb shanks with salt and pepper. In a large Dutch oven over medium-high heat, warm the oil. Working in batches to avoid crowding, add the shanks and sear, turning as needed with tongs, until golden brown on all sides, 8–10 minutes. Transfer to a plate.

Pour off most of the fat from the pot and return the pot to medium-high heat. Add the onion, cinnamon, cloves, and allspice and sauté until the onion is golden, about 7 minutes. Add the brandy and stir with a wooden spoon to dislodge any browned bits on the pan bottom. Stir in the tomatoes and broth, then add the lamb shanks and any juices that have collected on the plate. Cover, place in the oven, and cook until the meat is very tender, 2½–3 hours.

Transfer the shanks to a plate. Strain the braising liquid through a fine-mesh sieve into a small saucepan, let stand for a few minutes, and then skim away the fat from the surface with a large spoon. Bring to a boil over high heat and boil until reduced by about half, about 5 minutes. Pull the meat from the shanks and discard the bones. Shred the meat with 2 forks.

To serve, mound the shredded meat in a serving bowl or on individual plates and spoon some of the braising juices over the top. Garnish with the mint and pomegranate seeds and serve.

SERVES 6

BROCCOLI RABE WITH
GARLIC AND ANCHOVIES

It's never a hardship to eat your greens when they are flavored with a tempting combination of garlic and anchovies and drizzled with lemon juice. We give this same delicious treatment to lots of different vegetables—kale, asparagus, green beans, pea shoots, nettles, spinach, Swiss chard—and then serve them as a side to our favorite grilled meats.

INGREDIENTS

Salt and freshly ground black pepper

1½ lb (750 g) broccoli rabe, trimmed

4 Tbsp (2 fl oz/60 ml) extra-virgin olive oil

2 large cloves garlic, each cut lengthwise into 4 slices

2 olive oil–packed anchovy fillets

¼ tsp red pepper flakes

¼ lemon

TOOLS

chef's knife, large pot, colander, frying pan, slotted spoon

Bring a large pot full of salted water to a boil and add the broccoli rabe. Cook, testing often, until the stems are just tender but the tip of a knife still meets some resistance, 2–3 minutes. Drain in a colander and cool under cold running water. Drain and squeeze gently to remove the excess liquid.

In a frying pan over medium-high heat, warm 3 tablespoons of the olive oil. Add the garlic and cook, stirring occasionally, until golden on both sides, 2–3 minutes. Using a slotted spoon, transfer the garlic to a small plate and set aside.

Add the anchovies to the pan and reduce the heat to medium. Using a fork, mash the anchovies until they dissolve in the oil, about 1 minute. Add the broccoli rabe and toss to coat. Add the red pepper flakes and cook, stirring occasionally, until the greens are heated through, about 2 minutes. Transfer to a serving bowl.

Drizzle the greens with the remaining 1 tablespoon olive oil and then squeeze the lemon quarter over them. Taste and adjust the seasoning with salt and black pepper. Add the garlic slices, if desired, and serve.

SERVES 4

in the kitchen with

MOLLY WIZENBERG
and BRANDON PETTIT

Favorite special occasion meal
Two Dungeness crabs and a bottle of something sparkling.

Always on the table at mealtime
Maldon salt, a pepper grinder, coasters sewn by our friend Hannah, and some linen napkins that we got as a wedding present.

Go-to meal for company
Prawns in a skillet with sriracha, lemon zest, butter, and herbs. A loaf of sourdough. A roll of paper towels. White wine. A fruit crumble for dessert.

Secret culinary weapon
Vinegar. Just a bit can perk up a dish without you even knowing it's there.

Maintaining kitchen bliss as a couple
Divide and conquer. Each time you cook together, divvy up the responsibilities and tasks. That way, you both contribute to getting the job done, but there's no confusion or tripping over each other. Also: sharing a beer doesn't hurt.

Always in the fridge
Cheddar cheese, vermouth, peanut butter, jam, hot sauce, eggs, hummus.

Favorite kitchen tools
A sharp chef's knife and an abundance of dishtowels.

CRISPY ROSEMARY POTATOES TWO WAYS

Here, we boil potatoes until they are tender and then give them a wonderfully crispy texture by finishing them in either a hot oven or a hot frying pan. Choose the method that works best for you, depending on what else you are cooking at the same time.

INGREDIENTS

2 lb (1 kg) Yukon gold, Yellow Finn, or russet potatoes

Salt

¼ cup (2 fl oz/60 ml) extra-virgin olive oil

2 sprigs fresh rosemary (optional)

TOOLS

paring knife, large pot, colander, large mixing bowl (optional), rimmed baking sheets, chef's knife (optional), spatula, large cast-iron frying pan (optional)

If you will be roasting the potatoes, preheat the oven to 400°F (200°C).

Leaving the potatoes unpeeled, cut them into irregularly shaped pieces about 1 inch (2.5 cm) thick. Bring a large pot of salted water to a boil, add the potatoes, and reduce the heat to a simmer. Cook the potatoes until they are tender and a bit frayed at the edges but still retain their shape, about 10 minutes. Don't worry if the skins start to peel away and a few bits of potato break off. Drain the potatoes well.

To roast the potatoes, in a large bowl, toss the cooked potatoes with the olive oil to coat. Arrange the potatoes in a single layer (not touching) on baking sheets. Pick the leaves from the rosemary sprigs, coarsely chop, and sprinkle evenly over the potatoes. Season with 2 teaspoons salt. Roast for 10 minutes, then start turning the potatoes as they brown. Roast for 15 minutes more, occasionally rotating and flipping the potatoes so that they brown evenly on all sides. If the potatoes stick to the pan, loosen them with a metal spatula.

To panfry the potatoes, spread the boiled potatoes on a rimmed baking sheet to cool. In a large cast-iron frying pan over medium heat, warm the olive oil. Working in batches to avoid crowding, add a single layer of potatoes and cook for 8 minutes, flipping the potatoes as needed so they brown evenly. Continue cooking until the potatoes are golden on all sides, 6–8 minutes longer. Transfer to a plate and keep warm. Repeat with the remaining potatoes. Season the fried potatoes with 2 teaspoons salt.

Whichever method you choose, the potatoes can be served right away or held in a 250°F (120°C) oven for up to 20 minutes.

SERVES 4

ROASTED CAULIFLOWER
WITH LEMON AND OLIVES

In this recipe, mild cauliflower gets a flavor boost from a scattering of green olives and a dusting of tart lemon zest. If you can find it at the market, use Romanesco cauliflower (sometimes labeled Romanesco broccoli), which has beautifully spiraled lime green florets and a slightly sweeter flavor than white cauliflower.

INGREDIENTS

1 head cauliflower, about 1½ lb (750 g)

⅓ cup (3 fl oz/80 ml) extra-virgin olive oil

Grated zest of 1 lemon

½ cup (2½ oz/75 g) pitted green olives such as Cerignola, coarsely chopped

Salt and freshly ground pepper

TOOLS

rasp grater, chef's knife, shallow roasting pan

Preheat the oven to 400°F (200°C).

Trim the cauliflower and cut into 2-inch (5-cm) florets. In a shallow roasting pan large enough to hold the cauliflower pieces in a single layer, combine the cauliflower, olive oil, lemon zest, and olives. Season with salt and pepper and toss to mix well. Spread the ingredients in a single layer.

Roast the cauliflower, stirring occasionally, until browned and tender when pierced with a fork, about 15 minutes. Transfer to a serving dish and serve.

SERVES 4

ROASTED BEETS WITH
ORANGE AND HERBED GOAT CHEESE

Tangy, herby goat cheese and sweet, earthy beets are a match made in heaven. Use different colors of beets for visual appeal. If you're juggling dishes for a dinner menu, prepare the beets, dressing, and herbed goat cheese in advance and assemble at the last minute.

INGREDIENTS

1 orange

6 beets, about 1½ lb (750 g) total weight, greens removed

3 Tbsp extra-virgin olive oil

2 cloves garlic

Salt and freshly ground pepper

2 oz (60 g) fresh goat cheese

1½ tsp minced fresh chives

1½ tsp minced fresh flat-leaf parsley

½ tsp minced fresh tarragon

TOOLS

chef's knife, citrus zester, baking dish, paring knife, 2 small mixing bowls, citrus reamer or press, whisk

Preheat the oven to 400°F (200°C).

Finely shred the zest from the orange and set aside. Halve the orange, place half in a baking dish just large enough to hold it and the beets in a single layer, and set the other half aside. Add the beets and drizzle with 2 tablespoons of the olive oil. Add the garlic, sprinkle lightly with salt and pepper, and toss well. Cover the dish with foil and roast until the beets are tender when pierced with a paring knife, about 45 minutes. Remove the beets from the oven and let cool.

In a small bowl, mash together the goat cheese, chives, parsley, tarragon, and a pinch each of salt and pepper. Cover and refrigerate until ready to serve.

Remove the beets from the oven and let cool. Using the dull side of the paring knife, gently scrape the skins off the beets, then cut into a mix of narrow wedges and slices about ¼ inch (6 mm) thick. Arrange the beets on a platter.

Squeeze the juice from the roasted orange half into a small bowl and whisk in the remaining 1 tablespoon oil to make a dressing. Squeeze in more juice from the reserved fresh orange half, if desired, and let the dressing cool to room temperature.

Drizzle the beets lightly with the dressing, then sprinkle lightly with salt and pepper. Top the beets with small spoonfuls of the herbed goat cheese, garnish with the orange zest, and serve.

SERVES 4

CARDAMOM CRÈME BRÛLÉES

The distinctive flavors of cardamom and vanilla infuse these simple custards, which are ideally baked a day ahead of serving so they are fully chilled before you caramelize the lightly sugared tops. That way, the custard will still be cold when your guests break through the brittle top.

INGREDIENTS

2 cups (16 fl oz/500 ml) heavy cream

1 vanilla bean, split lengthwise

2 pods white cardamom, cracked open

6 large egg yolks

10 Tbsp (4½ oz/140 g) superfine sugar

Pinch of salt

TOOLS

paring knife, baking dish, four ¾-cup (6–fl oz/180-ml) ramekins, saucepan, mixing bowl, whisk, fine-mesh sieve, 2-cup (16–fl oz/500-ml) measuring pitcher, wire rack, rimmed baking sheet, kitchen torch (optional)

Preheat the oven to 325°F (165°C). Select a baking dish 2–2½ inches (5–6 cm) deep and large enough to hold four ¾-cup (6–fl oz/180-ml) ramekins or other ovenproof dishes. Line the baking dish with a thin kitchen towel.

In a saucepan over medium heat, combine the cream, vanilla bean, and cardamom pods and their seeds. Bring to a simmer and cook for 1 minute. Remove the vanilla bean and, using the tip of a knife, scrape the seeds into the cream. Continue to simmer the cream, stirring often, for another 3–4 minutes. Remove from the heat and let cool slightly.

In a bowl, whisk together the egg yolks, 6 tablespoons (3 oz/90 g) of the sugar, and the salt until thickened, about 2 minutes. Slowly add the warm (not hot) cream mixture, whisking constantly. Pour the custard through a fine-mesh sieve into a 2-cup measuring pitcher. Skim off any bubbles from the surface. Divide the custard evenly among the prepared ramekins. Place the ramekins in the towel-lined dish and pour hot water into the dish to reach halfway up the sides of the ramekins. Cover the dish loosely with foil.

Bake the custards until they are set but jiggle slightly in the center when shaken, 20–25 minutes. Transfer the baking dish to a wire rack, let the custards cool slightly, and then lift the ramekins out of the water bath and set on the rack to cool for 1 hour. Cover tightly and refrigerate for at least 3 hours and up to overnight.

When ready to serve, preheat the broiler. Sprinkle each custard evenly with 1 tablespoon each of the remaining sugar. Place the custards on a rimmed baking sheet and slide under the broiler about 4 inches (10 cm) from the heat source. Broil just until the sugar caramelizes, 1–2 minutes. (Alternatively, use a kitchen torch to caramelize the sugar.) Serve right away.

SERVES 4

RASPBERRIES IN LEMONGRASS SYRUP

This new spin on the classic pairing of berries and cream is an elegant and nearly effortless way to take advantage of an abundance of fresh, juicy raspberries in the market. You can also use 6 peaches, peeled and sliced, in place of the berries.

INGREDIENTS

1 stalk lemongrass

⅓ cup (3 oz/90 g) sugar

4 pt (2 lb/1 kg) raspberries

Sweetened whipped cream for serving

TOOLS

mixing bowl and whisk or electric mixer, chef's knife, small saucepan, fine-mesh sieve, large mixing bowl

Remove the dry outer leaves from the base of the lemongrass stalk and trim off the grassy tops, leaving the 3-inch (7.5-cm) base. Trim the roots off of the base. Using the back of the blade of a chef's knife, bruise the lemongrass, flattening the stalk and breaking some of the fibers to release its aroma.

In a small saucepan, combine the sugar and ⅓ cup (3 fl oz/80 ml) water and bring to a simmer over medium-high heat. Simmer, swirling occasionally, until the sugar is dissolved, about 2 minutes. Remove from the heat, add the lemongrass, cover, and let cool completely, about 30 minutes.

Strain the lemongrass syrup through a fine-mesh sieve into a large bowl, pressing on the stalk with the back of a spoon to extract as much syrup as possible; discard the lemongrass.

Add the raspberries to the syrup and stir gently. Divide the raspberries and syrup among individual bowls. Top with a dollop of whipped cream and serve.

SERVES 6

STRAWBERRY-RHUBARB GALETTE

Strawberries and rhubarb are a classic springtime combination. This recipe makes two galettes, but you can easily halve it for a smaller get-together. If you like, accompany each wedge with a small scoop of ice cream, crème fraîche, or whipped cream.

INGREDIENTS

10–12 rhubarb stalks, 1½–2 lb (750 g–1 kg) total weight, cut into ½-inch (12-mm) pieces

1 cup (8 oz/250 g) granulated sugar

2 sheets frozen puff pastry, about 9 oz (280 g) each, thawed according to package directions

4 pt (2 lb/1 kg) strawberries, hulled and quartered if large or halved if small

Confectioners' sugar for dusting

TOOLS

paring knife, chef's knife, rolling pin, 2 baking sheets, mixing bowl, 2 wire racks, fine-mesh sieve

In a saucepan, combine the rhubarb and ⅔ cup (5 oz/155 g) of the granulated sugar and let stand for 30 minutes.

Place the saucepan over medium heat and cook, stirring often, until the rhubarb is tender but not dissolving, 6–8 minutes. The rhubarb will release its juices. If it seems dry, add 2–3 teaspoons water. Remove from the heat and let cool.

Line 2 baking sheets with parchment paper. On a lightly floured work surface, roll out each puff pastry sheet into a 16-inch (40-cm) square, making sure there are no cracks in the pastry. Using a paring knife, cut off the corners of each square to make an uneven circle. Place each circle on a prepared baking sheet.

In a bowl, stir together the rhubarb and strawberries. Divide the rhubarb-strawberry mixture between the pastry circles, placing half in the center of each circle and leaving a 2-inch (5-cm) border uncovered. Divide the remaining ⅓ cup (3 oz/90 g) granulated sugar between the fruit-topped circles, sprinkling it evenly on top of the fruit. Fold the border over the fruit, pleating the edges to form a rim and covering all but about a 5-inch (13-cm) circle of fruit in the center of the pastry. Place in the freezer and chill for 20 minutes. Meanwhile, position 2 racks in the middle of the oven and preheat to 350°F (180°C).

Remove the baking sheets from the freezer and immediately place in the oven. Bake the galettes, rotating them 180 degrees at the midway point, until the crusts are puffed and golden brown, 20–25 minutes. Let cool for 10 minutes on the pans on wire racks. Transfer to a cutting board. Using a fine-mesh sieve, dust the galettes with the confectioners' sugar. Serve warm, cut into wedges.

SERVES 10–12

CHOCOLATE BROWNIE CAKE

The secret to this rich brownie cake is good-quality chocolate with a cacao content of at least 70 percent. Here, we call for dusting the cake with unsweetened cocoa powder, but confectioners' sugar is also good. For an extra flourish, accompany each slice with a dollop of whipped cream or a handful of fresh berries.

INGREDIENTS

½ cup (4 oz/125 g) butter, at room temperature, plus butter for pan

1 cup (8 oz/250 g) sugar

2 large eggs, lightly beaten

1 tsp vanilla extract

⅛ tsp salt

¾ cup (4 oz/125 g) all-purpose flour

4 oz (125 g) good-quality semisweet or bittersweet chocolate, coarsely chopped

Unsweetened cocoa powder for dusting

TOOLS

serrated knife, 8-inch (20-cm) round cake pan, large mixing bowl, electric mixer, saucepan and heatproof bowl or double boiler, silicone spatula, toothpick, wire rack, fine-mesh sieve

Preheat the oven to 350°F (180°C). Line an 8-inch (20-cm) round cake pan with a piece of foil, allowing the edge to hang over the pan rim. Using your fingers, lightly butter the foil.

In a large bowl, using an electric mixer on medium-high speed, beat the ½ cup butter until light and fluffy, about 1 minute. Add the sugar and beat until well blended. Add the eggs and vanilla and beat again until well blended. Add the salt and one-third of the flour and beat well. Add the remaining flour in two batches, beating well after each addition.

Fill a saucepan or the bottom pan of a double boiler with about 2 inches (5 cm) of water and bring to a bare simmer over medium-low heat. Put the chocolate in a heatproof bowl or the top of the double boiler and place over (not touching) the water. Heat the chocolate, stirring often with a silicone spatula, until melted. Remove from the heat and let cool slightly, 2–3 minutes. Add it to the cake batter and beat on medium speed until well blended and creamy.

Pour the batter into the prepared pan, smoothing the surface with the spatula. Bake until the cake is puffed and a toothpick inserted into the center comes out clean, 20–25 minutes. Transfer to a wire rack and let cool completely in the pan.

Using the edges of the foil, lift the cooled cake out of the pan. Invert the cake onto a cake stand or cake plate and peel off the foil. Turn the cake right side up. Using a fine-mesh sieve, dust the top with cocoa powder, cut into wedges, and serve.

SERVES 8–10

5

HOLIDAY FARE

HOLIDAY FARE

We view holidays as the perfect excuses for cooking an elaborate meal and drinking our treasured bottles of wine, two things we love to do.

Christie We love our families, but they live far away, so early in our marriage we found ourselves skipping airport crushes and instead spending the big holidays on our own or with a few friends.

Jordan Champagne is essential on Christmas. That's because it's perfect with caviar, our annual indulgence. We pull blini off the griddle, pile the briny roe on them, and enjoy them with bubbly as we open our gifts. A seafood course is next—say, scallops or turbot—something simple that tastes good with white wine. Then it is on to the main, which in recent years has been prime rib with Yorkshire pudding or leg of lamb, both of which call for a big red wine.

Christie Every holiday in our house involves a great spread, but Christmas dinner is invariably the most memorable. For many years running, we've been getting together with the same dear friends for the celebration, which always turns into a night that is best described as epic. We don't hold back on anything—time, food, or wine.

Jordan After dinner comes my favorite part of the ritual: we all put on a jacket, pour another glass of Champagne, and head out for a walk. Climbing the hill near our house brings us to a peak with a spectacular view. The millions of glimmering windows and street lamps of San Francisco become our Christmas lights, and we pause, reflecting on our lives as the lights reflect back on us. And then, our breath misting in the cold night air, we head home for dessert.

QUICK IDEAS *for* HOT DRINKS

Whether it's cookies, tarts, or pies—or even a savory cheese—we happily down holiday treats with spiced (and sometimes spiked) hot drinks. These beverages are festive and fun, equally good for a party and crowd or a quiet night a deux in front of the fire.

Because making hot drinks requires a little extra effort (they aren't as simple as mixing gin, vermouth, and ice), we often don't make them unless it's holiday season. But we also know that few things are as glowingly satisfying as a warm drink on a dreary day. So we have to remind ourselves that making hot drinks isn't really that difficult, as these six ideas prove.

MULLED CIDER
Warm apple cider + cinnamon stick + cloves + apple slices.

SPICED COFFEE
Brewed coffee + cinnamon sticks + cardamom pods.

SMOKY TODDY
Warm brewed Lapsang souchong tea + splash brandy + 2 pinches sugar + splash fresh lemon juice.

HOT BUTTERED RUM
Warm hot water + splash rum + heaping spoonful honey + small dab butter.

HOT CHOCOLATE
Warm milk + cocoa powder + grated bittersweet chocolate + pinch each sugar, salt, and ground cinnamon.

LEMON VERBENA–MINT TISANE
Warm hot water + handful each fresh lemon verbena and mint leaves.

QUICK IDEAS *for* COOKIES

At holiday time, one of us becomes a cookie-making fool. Every weekend, the kitchen is forfeited to this calling, with clouds of flour dust filling the air and cooling racks covering the counters. Most of the cookies are meant as gifts, but plenty of them manage to stick around, too.

Once you master a basic sugar cookie recipe, you can make your own customized cookies by cutting them into shapes and adding different flavors and colors. Around the holidays, we like to give friends our unique home-baked creations. Plus, making the cookies is a way for us to celebrate at home together before the craziness of the season begins.

BASIC SUGAR COOKIES

Cream 1¼ cups (10 oz/315 g) softened butter and ¾ cup (6 oz/185 g) sugar until fluffy. Beat in 1 large egg yolk and 2 tsp vanilla extract. Sift 2 cups (10 oz/315 g) flour and ¼ tsp salt over the butter mixture and stir until blended. Divide into 4 equal portions, shape each portion into a thick disk, wrap separately in plastic wrap, and refrigerate for at least 3 hours. Preheat the oven to 350°F (180°C). Butter 2 baking sheets or line with parchment paper. Place each dough disk between 2 sheets waxed paper and roll out ¼ inch (6 mm) thick. Cut into shapes with cookie cutters and transfer to the prepared baking sheets. Bake until lightly golden, 10–12 minutes. Cool on wire racks.

SALTY CHOCOLATE COOKIE VARIATION

Reduce the flour to 1¾ cups (9 oz/ 280 g) and add ½ cup (1½ oz/45 g) unsweetened Dutch-process cocoa powder; sprinkle cookies with flaky sea salt, such as Maldon, before baking.

OTHER COOKIE FLAVOR VARIATIONS

Substitute lemon extract, almond extract, or rum for the vanilla extract.

ROYAL ICING

Beat together 3 Tbsp meringue powder and 6 Tbsp (3 fl oz/90 ml) warm water until smooth. Add 4 cups (1 lb/500 g) confectioners' sugar and beat until blended; add more water as needed for a spreadable consistency. Mix in food coloring as desired. Spread icing onto cooled cookies and top with edible decorations.

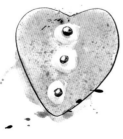
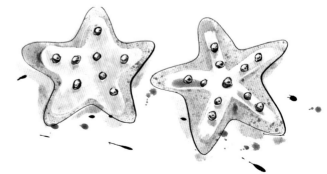

DATES TWO WAYS

In this easy, tasty holiday hors d'oeuvre, sweet, jammy dates pair beautifully with both tangy goat cheese and rich, creamy blue cheese. For added flavor, include a sliver of Spanish chorizo or other cooked spicy sausage in the stuffing, or wrap the stuffed dates with prosciutto and secure with a toothpick.

INGREDIENTS

30 small dates, preferably Deglet Noor or Medjool

¼ lb (125 g) semifirm Spanish goat's milk cheese, preferably *cabra al vino*

¼ lb (125 g) Gorgonzola or Cambozola cheese

Extra-virgin olive oil for drizzling

Flaky sea salt

TOOLS

paring knife, chef's knife

DRINK NOTE

Bursting with big, divergent flavors, this appetizer needs a full-fruited wine to match the dates, a perfect call for a rich, ripe red like California Zinfandel or Syrah. Other choices could include Côtes du Rhônes and other wines from southern France.

Using a sharp paring knife, cut a lengthwise slit in each date, from the top to the bottom, and remove the pit. Cut each type of cheese into 15 thin strips that will fit inside of a date.

Insert a strip of cheese into each date and press the slit closed. Arrange the dates on a platter. (The platter can be covered and left at room temperature for several hours before serving.)

Just before serving, drizzle the dates with olive oil.

MAKES 30 STUFFED DATES; SERVES 6–8

PROSCIUTTO-WRAPPED FIGS

Fresh figs have a short early-summer season and a second, longer season that stretches from late summer into late fall or early winter. Figs should be picked and purchased at their peak of ripeness, as they do not ripen further off the tree. Look for fragrant, moist-looking fruits that give slightly to gentle pressure.

INGREDIENTS

16 ripe figs such as Black Mission or Adriatic

8 paper-thin slices prosciutto

Aged balsamic vinegar for drizzling

TOOLS

paring knife, chef's knife

Trim the stem off of each fig, then cut or tear the fig in half lengthwise. Cut each slice of prosciutto into quarters. Wrap a piece of prosciutto around each fig half.

Arrange the wrapped figs on a serving platter. Drizzle with the balsamic vinegar and serve.

SERVES 8

SHRIMP COCKTAIL WITH BALSAMIC COCKTAIL SAUCE

Here, a hint of sweet balsamic vinegar moves traditional cocktail sauce upscale. The assertive mix is a tasty match with poached shrimp, but it also complements cooked crab or lobster or raw oysters on the half shell. Both the shrimp and the sauce can be prepared in advance, freeing you for other tasks as dinnertime approaches.

INGREDIENTS

FOR THE COCKTAIL SAUCE

1 tsp fresh lemon juice

⅔ cup (5 fl oz/160 ml) tomato ketchup

1–2 tsp prepared horseradish

1 tsp soy sauce

½ tsp balsamic vinegar

½ tsp Worcestershire sauce

¼ tsp dry mustard

Dash of hot-pepper sauce

1 lemon

½ tsp peppercorns

16–20 large shrimp in the shell, 1 lb (500 g) total weight

TOOLS

chef's knife, citrus reamer or press, assorted mixing bowls, whisk, large pot, colander, sharp paring knife

To make the cocktail sauce, in a small bowl, whisk together the lemon juice, ketchup, 1 teaspoon of the horseradish, the soy sauce, vinegar, Worcestershire sauce, mustard, and hot-pepper sauce until well blended. Taste and adjust with more horseradish and hot-pepper sauce if needed. Cover and let sit for at least 30 minutes to allow the flavors to blend, or refrigerate up to overnight.

Cut the lemon into quarters. Fill a large pot half full with water and add the lemon quarters and peppercorns. Bring to a boil over high heat, add the shrimp, cover, and bring back to a boil. Reduce the heat to medium and simmer for 1 minute; the shrimp should be just opaque. Drain into a colander and rinse under cold running water until cool.

To peel the shrimp, carefully pull off and discard the head if still attached. Then pull apart the legs and gently pull off the shell, working from the top to the tail and leaving the tail segments intact. Using a paring knife, cut a shallow channel in the back of the shrimp and pull away the dark veinlike tract with the tip of the knife. Put the shrimp in a bowl, cover, and refrigerate for at least 10 minutes or up to 6 hours.

To serve, arrange the chilled shrimp on a platter with the sauce alongside for dipping.

SERVES 4–6

RADICCHIO SALAD WITH
PEARS, WALNUTS, AND GOAT CHEESE

Radicchio's brilliant red hues matched with golden-, green-, or red-skinned pears make this a festive salad for the holidays. Goat cheese and walnuts accompany the radicchio here, but a mild blue and almonds or pistachios can be used in their place.

INGREDIENTS

½ cup (2 oz/60 g) walnuts

2 firm but ripe pears

1 Tbsp fresh lemon juice

2 heads radicchio

3 Tbsp extra-virgin olive oil

1 Tbsp balsamic vinegar

Salt and freshly ground pepper

6 oz (185 g) semi-aged goat cheese, such as *Bûcheron*, or fresh goat cheese, cut into 8 slices

TOOLS

chef's knife, citrus reamer or press, rimmed baking sheet, paring knife, assorted mixing bowls, whisk

Preheat the oven to 350°F (180°C). Spread the walnuts in a single layer on a rimmed baking sheet and bake, stirring once or twice, until fragrant and lightly toasted, 10–12 minutes. Pour onto a small plate and let cool, then chop coarsely.

Halve and core the pears, cut lengthwise into thin slices, and place in a bowl. Drizzle with the lemon juice, toss to coat, and set aside. Remove and discard any brown or wilted leaves from the radicchio heads, then separate the bright red leaves from the heads.

To make the dressing, in a small bowl, whisk together the olive oil, vinegar, and ¼ teaspoon salt until emulsified.

Place a few leaves of radicchio on each plate. Arrange the pear slices and cheese on top and sprinkle with the walnuts. Drizzle each salad plate evenly with the dressing, season with pepper, and serve.

SERVES 8

ARUGULA, FENNEL, AND ORANGE SALAD

The peppery bite of arugula, the anise accent of fennel, and the tangy sweetness of oranges come together in this vibrant winter salad. You can make the vinaigrette and prepare the fennel and oranges up to a day ahead and refrigerate them. Then, just before serving, bring all of the elements together.

INGREDIENTS

FOR THE VINAIGRETTE

2 tsp grated orange zest

¼ cup (2 fl oz/60 ml) fresh orange juice

2 Tbsp fresh lemon juice

2 Tbsp extra-virgin olive oil

2 Tbsp canola oil

2 tsp Dijon mustard

½ tsp dried tarragon

1 shallot, chopped

Salt and freshly ground pepper

3 large navel oranges

1 large fennel bulb

4 cups (4 oz/125 g) arugula

TOOLS

chef's knife, citrus reamer or press, rasp grater, small mixing bowl, whisk

To make the vinaigrette, in a small bowl, whisk together the orange zest, orange juice, lemon juice, olive oil, canola oil, mustard, tarragon, and shallot. Season to taste with salt and pepper. Set aside.

Working with 1 orange at a time, and using a sharp knife, cut a slice off both ends of the orange to reveal the flesh. Stand the orange upright and, using the knife, cut downward to remove the peel and pith in thick strips, following the contour of the fruit. Cut the orange in half crosswise, place each half cut side down, and thinly slice vertically to create half-moons. Repeat with the remaining oranges.

Cut off the stems and feathery fronds of the fennel bulb and remove any bruised or discolored outer layers. Cut the bulb in half lengthwise and cut out any tough core parts. Cut the bulb halves crosswise into thin slices.

Place the fennel and arugula in a large serving bowl, add half of the vinaigrette, and toss gently to coat thoroughly. Arrange the orange slices on top. Drizzle with the remaining vinaigrette and serve.

SERVES 8–10

BUTTERNUT SQUASH SOUP
WITH GINGER CRÈME FRAÎCHE

Roasting enhances the sweetness of winter squash and caramelizes garlic cloves, which gives this silky smooth soup a particularly complex flavor. The ginger-spiced crème fraîche cuts the richness and has a pleasant cooling effect. The soup is a memorable first course for Thanksgiving or Christmas dinner.

INGREDIENTS

2 butternut, acorn, or delicata squashes, 5–6 lb (2.5–3 kg) total weight

2 Tbsp butter, melted, plus 4 Tbsp (2 oz/60 g)

Salt and freshly ground black pepper

1 head garlic, cloves separated

4 sprigs fresh thyme

4 sprigs fresh rosemary

FOR THE GINGER CRÈME FRAÎCHE

1 cup (8 oz/250 g) crème fraîche

1 Tbsp peeled and grated fresh ginger

⅛ tsp sugar

Pinch of salt

1 cup (5 oz/155 g) chopped shallots

4 cups (32 fl oz/1 l) chicken broth

¾ cup (6 fl oz/180 ml) dry white wine

1 cup (8 fl oz/250 ml) heavy cream

1 tsp freshly grated nutmeg

⅛ tsp cayenne pepper

TOOLS

chef's knife, rasp grater, nutmeg grater (optional), pastry brush, rimmed baking sheet, paring knife, assorted mixing bowls, large pot, immersion blender or blender or food processor, ladle

Preheat the oven to 375°F (190°C). Cut each squash in half lengthwise and scoop out the seeds with a spoon. Brush the cut surfaces of the squash halves with the 2 tablespoons melted butter, then sprinkle with ½ teaspoon each salt and black pepper. Stuff the cavities with the unpeeled garlic cloves and 1 sprig each of the thyme and rosemary, then carefully turn the squash halves cut side down on a rimmed baking sheet. Bake until very tender when pierced with a paring knife, 45–50 minutes. Set aside to cool.

While the squashes are cooking, make the ginger crème fraîche. In a small bowl, stir together the crème fraîche, ginger, sugar, and salt until well blended. Cover and refrigerate.

When the squash halves are cool enough to handle, remove the garlic and herbs and discard the herbs, but set the garlic aside. Scoop the squash flesh into a bowl. Squeeze the roasted garlic from its skin into the same bowl. In a large pot over medium-high heat, melt the remaining 4 tablespoons butter. Add the shallots and cook, stirring often, until soft, 3–4 minutes. Add the squash and garlic to the pot and, using the back of a spoon, mash all the ingredients together. Stir in the broth and wine and bring to a simmer. Stir in the cream and remove from the heat.

Using an immersion blender, blender, or food processor, purée the soup, then return to the pot if necessary. Add the nutmeg, cayenne, 1 tablespoon salt, and ¼ teaspoon black pepper and reheat gently to serving temperature. Taste and adjust the seasoning.

To serve, ladle the soup into bowls, add a dollop of the ginger crème fraîche, and serve.

SERVES 8

WHAT'S A FAVORITE HOLIDAY DISH YOU LIKE TO MAKE?

Molly and Brandon

I make a pecan-and-chocolate pie that's been in my family for years. We call it Hoosier Pie. Brandon is famous for his mashed potatoes with roasted garlic and Parmesan. And we both love Brussels sprouts, so they're always on our holiday table—either shredded and sautéed, or braised in cream.

Mindy and Daniel

Dan's family always shares a big pot of soup on Christmas Eve, so every year he cooks it. I make wild mushroom brioche stuffing at Thanksgiving. I have a cousin who has made the same stuffing since 1965. Two years ago she finally passed the job on to me.

Lisa and Emmett

We love Thanksgiving. Emmett roasts the turkey, quickly, using high heat, and it always comes out perfect. He makes gravy from the drippings plus giblets, wine, roasted celery, onion, and carrots. He skims off the fat then purees the gravy in the blender with his secret ingredient...the fresh turkey liver! It comes out rich and smooth. I like to reinterpret classic side dishes and always make a fresh cranberry sauce made with ginger beer.

Aki and Alex

Grandma Kitty's strawberry pie is a staple at Easter time. There is no substitute.

Andrea and Mac

We love to make oysters Rockefeller before Thanksgiving dinner.

Julie and Matt

One Thanksgiving we were charged with pies. We had just barely learned how to make a good crust and weren't yet comfortable with baking. Our kitchen was a crazy, flour-covered mess and we were up all night fretting over these pies. Now we love to bake them.

SEARED SCALLOPS WITH WARM BACON VINAIGRETTE

Frisée, a curly-edged, hearty chicory variety, stands up well to a warm dressing like this smoky bacon vinaigrette laced with Dijon mustard and sherry vinegar. Top the greens with rich, buttery scallops, and you'll have a salad worthy of a special occasion.

INGREDIENTS

8 slices bacon

⅔ cup plus 2 Tbsp (6 fl oz/190 ml) extra-virgin olive oil, plus more as needed

1 cup (5 oz/155 g) finely chopped shallots

4 cloves garlic, minced

2 Tbsp Dijon mustard

6 Tbsp (3 fl oz/90 ml) sherry vinegar

2 Tbsp sugar

Salt and freshly ground pepper

24 large sea scallops, about 1½ lb (750 g) total weight

1 lb (500 g) frisée, torn into bite-sized pieces

TOOLS

chef's knife, large sauté pan, tongs, large mixing bowl, whisk, frying pan

DRINK NOTE

A dish of this caliber deserves a great wine that's perfectly tailored to it: Chardonnay. Splurge on a superior white Burgundy from an appellation like Meursault, Puligny-Montrachet, or Chassagne-Montrachet, with a creamy texture to complement the satiny scallops and a little toast to bring out the bacon. A lightly oaked Chardonnay from California or Oregon would work, too.

In a large sauté pan over medium-high heat, fry the bacon until crisp, about 5 minutes. Transfer to paper towels to drain. When the bacon is cool enough to handle, crumble it into a large bowl and set aside. Drain off all but 3 tablespoons of the bacon fat from the pan. If you have less than 3 tablespoons, supplement with olive oil.

Return the pan with the fat to medium heat. Add the shallots and sauté until lightly browned, 2–3 minutes. Add the garlic and cook for another minute. Remove from the heat and whisk in the mustard, vinegar, ⅔ cup (5 fl oz/155 ml) of the olive oil, and the sugar to make a vinaigrette. Season to taste with salt and pepper.

Remove the tough muscle from the side of each scallop if necessary. Pat the scallops dry and season with salt and pepper. Heat 1½ teaspoons of the olive oil in a frying pan over medium-high heat. Arrange 6 of the scallops in the pan without crowding and sauté, turning once, until golden and just cooked through, 1–2 minutes per side. Transfer the scallops to a plate. Repeat 3 more times, adding another 1½ teaspoons olive oil and another 6 scallops each time.

Add the frisée to the bowl with the bacon. Reheat the vinaigrette over low heat until warm, about 1 minute. Pour three-fourths of the vinaigrette over the greens and toss to coat. Divide the salad evenly among individual plates. Top with the scallops, drizzle with the remaining vinaigrette, and serve.

SERVES 8

ROAST BEEF WITH YORKSHIRE PUDDING

This classic recipe is ideal for the first holiday feast you host as a married couple because it is both impressive and easy to prepare. Plan on roasting the beef for 15 minutes per pound (500 g). The Yorkshire pudding, which is like a giant popover, takes advantage of the fat from the roast, so it bakes while the roast rests. You may want to make a double batch of the pudding—everybody likes it!

INGREDIENTS

FOR THE ROAST BEEF

5 lb (2.5 kg) beef rib or sirloin tip roast

Salt and freshly ground pepper

FOR THE YORKSHIRE PUDDING

2 large eggs

1¼ cups (10 fl oz/310 ml) whole milk

¾ cup plus 2 Tbsp (4½ oz/140 g) all-purpose flour

Salt

TOOLS

large roasting pan, bulb baster (optional), instant-read thermometer, carving board, 9-inch (23-cm) cast-iron frying pan or Pyrex pie dish, mixing bowl, whisk, chef's knife

DRINK NOTE

Break out that expensive bottle of Cabernet for this juicy roast beef. Its dark cherry and cassis flavors merge effortlessly with the perfectly cooked beef, while its tannins help cut through the richness of the meat. Look for a big wine from the Napa Valley, South Africa, Chile, Argentina, or, of course, Bordeaux.

One day before serving, season the roast with 2½ teaspoons salt and several grinds of pepper. Cover and refrigerate overnight. Remove the roast from the refrigerator 1–2 hours before it is scheduled to go into the oven to allow it to lose its chill.

To roast the beef, preheat the oven to 425°F (220°C). Place the beef in a large roasting pan and place in the oven. Roast for 15 minutes, then reduce the heat to 375°F (190°C). Continue to roast, basting the meat frequently with the pan juices, until an instant-read thermometer inserted into the center of the roast away from any bones registers 135°F (57°C) for medium-rare, about 1¼ hours. (If using a boneless roast, start checking the temperature a little earlier.) Transfer the roast to a carving board and let rest, tented with foil, for 30 minutes. Reserve the roasting pan with the drippings and keep the oven on. While the roast rests, make the Yorkshire pudding.

To make the Yorkshire pudding, place a 9-inch (23-cm) cast-iron frying pan or Pyrex pie dish in the oven to preheat. Meanwhile, in a bowl, whisk together the eggs and milk until blended. Add the flour, a little at a time, whisking constantly until smooth. The batter should have the consistency of heavy cream. Add a pinch of salt. Remove the frying pan from the oven and transfer 2 tablespoons of the beef fat from the roasting pan to the frying pan. (Tilt the roasting pan and spoon off the clear fat from the brown drippings.) Pour the batter into the hot pan and place in the oven. Bake until the pudding is puffy and crisp, about 25 minutes.

To serve, carve the roast beef into slices and cut the pudding into wedges.

SERVES 8

ROASTED SALT-BRINED TURKEY WITH SAGE

Roasting a turkey isn't as daunting as it can seem, especially if you follow a few tricks to keep the meat moist. We soak the bird overnight in a salt, sugar, and herb brine, coat it with butter before it goes in the oven, and then baste it with a butter-oil mix every hour to keep it succulent.

INGREDIENTS

3 cups (1½ lb/750 g) kosher salt

½ cup (4 oz/125 g) sugar

1 small yellow onion, chopped

1 bunch fresh thyme

1 Tbsp peppercorns, cracked

1 fresh turkey, about 14 lb (7 kg), giblets and any excess fat removed

4 Tbsp (2 oz/60 g) unsalted butter, at room temperature, plus 4 Tbsp, melted

1 bunch fresh sage

Freshly ground pepper

½ cup (4 fl oz/125 ml) olive oil

Classic Gravy (page 214)

TOOLS

chef's knife, large pot or brining bag, kitchen twine, V-shaped roasting rack, large roasting pan, small mixing bowl, bulb baster, instant-read thermometer, carving board

DRINK NOTE

The subject of pairing wine and turkey is a source of many great debates. Some folks prefer whites, like a fruity Riesling or an aromatic Gewürztraminer. Others insist on light reds, such as Beaujolais or Pinot Noir. We like them all, though we admit to a special fondness for earthy Syrah from the Rhône Valley or Northern California.

Choose a pot that is large enough to hold the turkey and will fit inside your refrigerator, or use a brining bag. Fill the pot one-third full with cold water. Stir in the salt, sugar, onion, thyme, and peppercorns. Add the turkey, breast side down, and fill with more water so it reaches as far above the turkey as possible. Cover with the lid and refrigerate for 24 hours.

Two hours before roasting, remove the turkey from the brine, discard the brine, and rinse the turkey inside and out under cold running water and pat dry with paper towels inside and out.

To roast the turkey, position a rack in the lower third of the oven and preheat to 425°F (220°C). Carefully slide your fingers between the skin and breast to loosen the skin. Spread half of the room-temperature butter on the breast meat under the skin, then insert about 12 large sage leaves under the skin, spacing them evenly. Season the neck and body cavities with pepper. Place the remaining sage sprigs in the cavity.

Tuck the wings under the bird and tie the legs together. Rub the bird with the remaining softened butter, then place, breast side up, on a V-shaped rack in a large roasting pan. Pour water to a depth of 1 inch (2.5 cm) into the bottom of the pan. In a small bowl, combine the melted butter and olive oil to use for basting.

Reduce the oven temperature to 325°F (165°C) and roast the turkey for 3–3½ hours, basting every hour with the butter mixture. Begin testing for doneness after 2½ hours. An instant-read thermometer inserted into the thickest part of the thigh away from the bone should register 170°F (77°C). Transfer the turkey to a carving board, tent with foil, and lest rest for 30 minutes before carving. Reserve the roasting pan with the drippings to make the gravy (see page 214).

SERVES 8–10

CLASSIC GRAVY

To make it easier to remove the fat from the pan drippings, once you pour the drippings into a measuring pitcher, put the pitcher in the freezer for 10–15 minutes. The fat will rise to the top and begin to congeal, making it easy to scoop off the fat without stealing the flavorful juices below.

INGREDIENTS

Pan drippings from
roasted turkey (page 213)

⅓ cup (2 oz/60 g)
all-purpose flour

½ cup (4 fl oz/125 ml)
dry white vermouth

About 1½ cups (12 fl oz/
375 ml) chicken broth

Salt and freshly ground
pepper

TOOLS

large glass measuring pitcher,
whisk, wooden spoon

Pour the drippings from the roasting pan into a large glass measuring pitcher. Let stand for at least 10 minutes to allow the fat to rise to the surface, then spoon off all of the fat, reserving ¼ cup (2 fl oz/60 ml) of it. Return the reserved fat to the roasting pan. Leave the drippings in the pitcher.

Place the roasting pan over 2 burners and turn on the heat to medium. Whisk in the flour and cook, whisking constantly, for 2–3 minutes. Add the vermouth and stir with a wooden spoon to scrape up the browned bits from the pan bottom. Add enough broth to the drippings to make 2 cups (16 fl oz/500 ml) and pour into the pan. Cook, stirring frequently, until the gravy thickens, about 5 minutes. Add more broth, if needed, to thin out the gravy, and season to taste with salt and pepper.

Pour into a gravy boat or small serving pitcher and serve alongside the roasted turkey.

MAKES ABOUT 2 CUPS (16 FL OZ/500 ML)

FRESH CRANBERRY RELISH

This tangy-sweet condiment couldn't be easier to make: you just finely mince everything in a food processor. We leave both the orange and the apple unpeeled for extra texture and flavor. Let the relish rest for at least a couple of days before serving to allow the flavors to mellow.

INGREDIENTS

1 small orange

1 small tart apple such as Granny Smith

2 cups (8 oz/250 g) fresh cranberries

⅓ cup (3 oz/90 g) sugar

1 thick slice peeled fresh ginger

TOOLS

paring knife, chef's knife, food processor

Quarter the unpeeled orange and remove any seeds. Cut the orange into 1-inch (2.5-cm) pieces. Quarter and core the unpeeled apple and cut it into 1-inch (2.5-cm) chunks.

In a food processor, combine the orange, apple, cranberries, sugar, and ginger, and process until finely minced. Transfer to an airtight container, cover, and store in the refrigerator for up to 2 weeks.

SERVES 6–8

BEEF TENDERLOIN WITH
SHALLOT AND RED WINE REDUCTION

The tenderloin is both the most tender and the most expensive cut of beef. It is also leaner than many other cuts, which means it needs relatively brief cooking and tastes best when cooked to no more than medium-rare. The red wine reduction, made from the flavorful pan juices, is quickly assembled while the roast rests.

INGREDIENTS

1 beef tenderloin,
2½–3 lb (1.25–1.5 kg)

2 Tbsp extra-virgin
olive oil

2 tsp minced fresh
thyme

Salt and freshly ground
pepper

2 Tbsp minced shallots

1 cup (8 fl oz/250 ml)
full-bodied red wine
such as Syrah or
Cabernet Sauvignon

2½ Tbsp butter

TOOLS

chef's knife, V-shaped roasting rack,
shallow roasting pan, instant-read thermometer,
carving board, wooden spoon

Remove the tenderloin from the refrigerator about 1 hour before it is scheduled to go in the oven to allow it to lose its chill.

Preheat the oven to 450°F (230°C). Rub the beef all over with the olive oil, then rub with the thyme, 1½ teaspoons salt, and 1 teaspoon pepper.

Place the roast on a V-shaped rack in a shallow roasting pan just large enough to accommodate it. Roast until an instant-read thermometer inserted into the thickest part of the tenderloin registers 115°–120°F (46°–49°C) for rare, about 20 minutes; 125°–130°F (52°–54°C) for medium-rare, about 25 minutes; or 130°–140°F (54°–60°C) for medium, about 30 minutes.

When the roast has reached the desired degree of doneness, transfer to a carving board and tent loosely with foil. Let rest for about 15 minutes.

Meanwhile, remove the rack from the roasting pan and place the pan on the stove top over medium heat. Add the shallots and sauté, stirring them into the pan juices, until translucent, about 2 minutes. Add the wine, a little at a time, stirring and scraping up any browned bits with a wooden spoon from the pan bottom. Continue to cook until the wine is reduced by nearly half. Stir in the butter. When the butter has melted, remove from the heat and cover to keep warm.

To serve, cut the beef across the grain into slices ½ inch (12 mm) thick. Arrange the slices on a platter, drizzle with the sauce, and serve.

SERVES 8

ROAST LEG OF LAMB WITH
GARLIC, HERBS, AND RED WINE

This tender, fragrant roast is prepared in the Greek style, with mashed garlic, herbs, and red pepper flakes packed into slits in the meat. Do not be tempted to cook it beyond medium, or it will lose its succulent texture. Serve with herb-roasted red potatoes or garlic mashed potatoes (opposite).

INGREDIENTS

1 clove garlic

Salt and freshly ground black pepper

1 Tbsp dried oregano

1 Tbsp minced fresh rosemary

⅛ tsp red pepper flakes

2 Tbsp extra-virgin olive oil

1 bone-in, shank-end half leg of lamb, about 5 lb (2.5 kg)

½ cup (4 fl oz/125 ml) dry red wine

TOOLS

chef's knife, mortar and pestle, paring knife, V-shaped roasting rack, roasting pan, instant-read thermometer, carving board

DRINK NOTE

We like to accompany lamb with a gamy, meaty Syrah from (or made in the style of) the northern Rhône appellations, such as Cornas or Côte-Rôtie. But we have also found, rather unexpectedly, that the brash berry flavors of Pinot Noir marry nicely with the grassy flavors of lamb. Look for a stout-bodied Pinot from California's Sonoma coast or Santa Barbara or from Oregon or Burgundy.

In a mortar, using a pestle, mash the garlic with ½ teaspoon salt. Add the oregano, rosemary, and red pepper flakes and mash to blend. Add the olive oil and work it in until the mixture is well combined.

Using a paring knife, cut 16 slits about ¾ inch (2 cm) deep all over the lamb. Rub some of the herb paste into each slit, then rub the meat all over with the remaining herb paste. Place the lamb in a large resealable plastic bag and pour in the wine. Seal the bag and massage the meat to coat it with the wine. Refrigerate for 24 hours.

When ready to roast the lamb, preheat the oven to 450°F (230°C). Place a V-shaped rack in a roasting pan just large enough to hold the lamb comfortably.

Remove the lamb from the plastic bag and pat dry with paper towels. Season lightly with salt and black pepper. Place the meat, fat side down, on the rack. Roast for 20 minutes. Turn the meat fat side up, reduce the heat to 375°F (190°C), and roast until an instant-read thermometer inserted into the thickest part away from the bone registers 115°–120°F (46°–49°C) for rare, about 30 minutes longer; 125°–130°F (52°–54°C) for medium-rare, 50–60 minutes longer; or 140°F (60°C) for medium, about 1¼ hours longer.

Transfer the lamb to a carving board and let rest for 15 minutes. Meanwhile, pour the pan juices into a gravy boat, let sit for 10 minutes, and skim off as much fat as possible. Carve the lamb, arrange the slices on a platter or individual plates, and serve. Pass the pan juices at the table.

SERVES 6–8

MASHED YUKON GOLD POTATOES
WITH GARLIC AND CHIVES

With their golden color and buttery flavor, Yukon gold potatoes are excellent mashed and seasoned with garlic and chives. A quick sauté softens the heat of the garlic to a gentle sweetness. You can make the mashed potatoes up to 2 hours in advance and reheat them in a heatproof bowl or the top pan of a double boiler placed over simmering water.

INGREDIENTS

3½ lb (1.75 kg) large Yukon gold potatoes, peeled and cut into large chunks

Salt and freshly ground pepper

4 Tbsp (2 oz/60 g) butter, at room temperature

8 large cloves garlic, minced

1 cup (8 fl oz/250 ml) whole milk

⅓ cup (½ oz/15 g) minced fresh chives

TOOLS

vegetable peeler, chef's knife, large pot, 2 small saucepans, colander, potato masher, wooden spoon

In a large pot, combine the potatoes, 1 tablespoon salt, and water to cover and bring to a simmer over medium-high heat. Reduce the heat to medium-low, cover, and simmer until the potatoes are tender when pierced with a fork, about 30 minutes.

While the potatoes are cooking, in a small saucepan over low heat, melt 2 tablespoons of the butter. Add the garlic and sauté just until it turns translucent, 1–2 minutes. Do not let it brown. Set aside.

In another small saucepan over medium-low heat, warm the milk until bubbles appear along the sides of the pan. Set aside and keep warm.

When the potatoes are ready, drain them, reserving about ⅓ cup (3 fl oz/80 ml) of the cooking liquid.

Return the potatoes to the pot and place over low heat. Mash thoroughly with a potato masher. Using a wooden spoon, gradually stir in half of the warm milk, the remaining 2 tablespoons butter, the sautéed garlic, and the chives. Add the remaining milk and, if necessary, the reserved cooking liquid, adding just enough to achieve the desired consistency. Stir until light and fluffy. Do not overmix, or the potatoes will turn gummy. Season to taste with salt and pepper. Transfer to a serving bowl and serve.

SERVES 6–8

ROASTED ACORN SQUASH
WITH CHIPOTLE AND CILANTRO

In this bold-flavored autumn recipe, aromatic cilantro, tart lime juice, and spicy, smoky chipotle chiles help cut through the sweetness and creaminess of the roasted squash. The result is a balanced, not-too-spicy dish of layered flavors.

INGREDIENTS

4 acorn squashes, about 6 lb (3 kg) total weight

4 limes

6 Tbsp (3 fl oz/90 ml) extra-virgin olive oil

2 chipotle chiles in adobo sauce, plus 2 tsp adobo sauce

1 tsp sugar

Salt and freshly ground pepper

¼ cup (⅓ oz/10 g) coarsely chopped fresh cilantro

TOOLS

chef's knife, citrus reamer or press, 2 large mixing bowls, 2 rimmed baking sheets, sharp paring knife

Preheat the oven to 425°F (220°C).

Cut each squash in half, then scoop out and discard the seeds. Cut each half into crescent-shaped wedges about ¾ inch (2 cm) thick.

Halve 2 of the limes and squeeze the juice into a large bowl. Add the olive oil, adobo sauce, sugar, and a generous pinch each of salt and pepper and stir well. Add the squash wedges to the bowl and toss to coat evenly. Pour the wedges and their juices onto 2 rimmed baking sheets and arrange them in a single layer.

Roast, turning the wedges once, until golden brown and tender when pierced with a sharp knife, about 25 minutes.

While the squash is roasting, remove the seeds from the chipotle chiles, then mince.

Transfer the squash wedges to a large bowl. Add the minced chile and the cilantro and toss to coat evenly. Arrange the squash on a platter, squeeze the juice from the remaining limes over the squash, and serve.

SERVES 8

PARSNIPS AND SWEET POTATOES
WITH HAZELNUTS AND BROWN BUTTER

The deep flavors of toasted nuts and brown butter pair well with earthy root vegetables. Both parsnips and sweet potatoes are high in natural sugars, which caramelize in the heat of the oven. The addition of thyme makes this side dish a particularly good partner to roasted poultry.

INGREDIENTS

½ cup (2½ oz/75 g) hazelnuts

6 Tbsp (3 fl oz/90 ml) canola oil

4 parsnips, about 2 lb (1 kg) total weight

2 sweet potatoes, about 2 lb (1 kg) total weight

Salt and freshly ground pepper

¼ cup (2 oz/60 g) butter

2 tsp minced fresh thyme

TOOLS

chef's knife, 2 small frying pans, 2 rimmed baking sheets, vegetable peeler

In a small, dry frying pan over medium-low heat, toast the hazelnuts, stirring often, until they turn a deep brown and are fragrant, 3–5 minutes. While the nuts are still warm, wrap them in a clean kitchen towel and rub them vigorously between your palms to remove the skins; it is fine if some bits of skin remain. Chop coarsely and set aside.

Preheat the oven to 425°F (220°C). Drizzle 1½ tablespoons of the oil onto each of 2 rimmed baking sheets and place in the oven to preheat while you prepare the vegetables.

Peel the parsnips and sweet potatoes, and cut into pieces about ½ inch (12 mm) thick and 2–3 inches (5–7.5 cm) long. Remove the baking sheets from the oven and divide the vegetables evenly between them. Sprinkle the vegetables lightly with salt and pepper, toss to coat evenly with the warm oil, and then spread them out in a single layer. Roast until the undersides are nicely browned and crisp, 10–12 minutes. Turn each piece and roast until the vegetables are browned on all sides, 8–10 minutes longer.

In a small frying pan over medium heat, melt the butter and cook, stirring occasionally, until it begins to turn brown and smell nutty, 3–4 minutes. Remove the pan from the heat and stir in the hazelnuts and thyme.

Transfer the roasted vegetables to a serving bowl, drizzle with the browned butter mixture, and toss gently to coat evenly. Taste and adjust the seasoning and serve.

SERVES 8

VINEGAR-GLAZED BRUSSELS SPROUTS WITH CHESTNUTS AND WALNUT OIL

The key to delicious Brussels sprouts is to brown them well to caramelize them, transforming their flavor from vegetal to nutty, before adding any liquid. A little fat from the butter, extra nuttiness from the chestnuts and walnut oil, and light pungency from the vinegar round out the flavors of this dish.

INGREDIENTS

2 lb (1 kg) Brussels sprouts

2 Tbsp extra-virgin olive oil

Salt and freshly ground pepper

2 Tbsp butter

2 cups (16 fl oz/500 ml) chicken broth

1 cup (about 6 oz/185 g) vacuum-packed whole chestnuts, coarsely chopped

2 Tbsp firmly packed light brown sugar

¼ cup (2 fl oz/60 ml) red wine vinegar

4 tsp walnut oil

TOOLS

chef's knife, paring knife, large frying pan, wooden spoon

Trim the stem ends of the Brussels sprouts and remove and discard any blemished or discolored leaves.

In a large frying pan over medium-high heat, warm the olive oil. When the oil is hot, add the Brussels sprouts and sprinkle lightly with salt. Cook, stirring occasionally, until golden brown and caramelized on all sides, about 4 minutes.

Raise the heat to medium-high and add the butter, broth, and chestnuts. Bring the broth to a boil and, using a wooden spoon, scrape up any browned bits from the pan bottom. Reduce the heat to medium-low, cover partially, and simmer until the sprouts are just tender when pierced with a sharp knife and most of the liquid has evaporated, 20–22 minutes.

Add ½ cup (4 fl oz/125 ml) water to the pan, stir in the sugar and vinegar, and raise the heat to medium-high. Cook, stirring occasionally, until the liquid reduces to a glaze, 2–3 minutes. Remove the pan from the heat and stir in the walnut oil. Season to taste with salt and pepper. Transfer to a serving bowl and serve.

SERVES 8

in the kitchen with

LISA and EMMETT FOX

Favorite wine or cocktail

All things bubbly. All Italian wines. An anejo manhattan (Lisa) and Blanton's with one big ice cube (Emmett).

Go-to meal for company

We love to cook paella on our "custom" outdoor grill (cinder blocks with wire grates). It's great for any number, we just change up the size of the pan and the ingredients. It's fun to make and always a crowd pleaser.

Maintaining kitchen bliss as a couple

Don't critique the way your partner cooks—especially if cooking for you!

Time-saving secret

Our pressure cooker. It cooks dried beans in a quarter of the time and they come out consistent and creamy. It's also great for quick steel-cut oatmeal.

Always on the table during meals

Lots of opened and unopened wine—and a corkscrew.

On setting the table

We use a runner instead of a tablecloth and oversized vintage white linen napkins; small vases of flowers, groupings of votives, and a few cellars of salt.

Favorite home-cooked meal for two

Roasted whole chicken, potato mashers, and lots of greens.

MUSHROOM AND POTATO GRATIN
WITH THYME AND PARMESAN

Hearty, comforting, and delicious, this dish is sure to become a holiday staple, whether served alongside beef tenderloin on Christmas or roasted turkey on Thanksgiving. Using a mixture of wild and cultivated mushrooms, such as chanterelle, cremini, and white button, gives this gratin a deep earthiness that enhances the buttery Yukon gold potatoes.

INGREDIENTS

1 Tbsp butter, plus more for dish

1½ cups (12 fl oz/375 ml) heavy cream

1 clove garlic, thinly sliced

3 sprigs fresh thyme, plus 1½ tsp minced

Salt and freshly ground pepper

2 lb (1 kg) Yukon gold potatoes

1 Tbsp extra-virgin olive oil

1 lb (500 g) mixed wild and cultivated mushrooms, woody stems removed and caps thinly sliced

5 Tbsp (1 oz/30 g) freshly grated Parmesan cheese

TOOLS

chef's knife, rasp grater, 8-inch (20-cm) square or 2-qt (2-l) oval baking dish or pan, large saucepan, vegetable peeler, mandoline (optional), frying pan, fine-mesh sieve

Preheat the oven to 375°F (190°C). Butter an 8-inch (20-cm) square or 2-qt (2-l) oval baking dish or pan.

In a large saucepan over medium heat, combine the cream, garlic, thyme sprigs, and a pinch each of salt and pepper and bring to a low boil. Remove from the heat and set aside.

Peel the potatoes and, using a mandoline or chef's knife, cut them into slices about ⅛ inch (3 mm) thick. Gently stir the potato slices into the cream mixture, cover, and let stand while you cook the mushrooms.

In a frying pan over medium heat, warm the olive oil and the 1 tablespoon butter until the butter melts and the mixture is hot. Add the mushrooms and a pinch of salt and sauté until all of the liquid released by the mushrooms has evaporated, 7–9 minutes. Add the minced thyme and a pinch of pepper and cook for 1 minute.

Arrange one-third of the potato slices, slightly overlapping, on the bottom of the prepared baking dish. Sprinkle lightly with salt and pepper and 1 tablespoon of the Parmesan. Spread half of the mushrooms over the potatoes and sprinkle with another 1 tablespoon Parmesan. Repeat these layers, using half of the remaining potatoes and all of the remaining mushrooms and sprinkling salt, pepper, and 1 tablespoon of the Parmesan between the layers. Top with the remaining potatoes and sprinkle with salt and pepper.

Pour the cream mixture through a fine-mesh sieve into the dish and sprinkle with the remaining 1 tablespoon Parmesan. Cover the dish with foil and bake until the potatoes are tender when pierced with a sharp knife, about 45 minutes. Remove the foil and bake until the top is golden brown, about 20 minutes longer. Let rest for about 10 minutes, then serve.

SERVES 6

GREEN BEANS WITH BACON
AND ONION VINAIGRETTE

Green beans are a common sight on the holiday table, but rarely do they taste this amazing. The beans are cooked until just tender and then tossed with salty, crispy bacon and a full-flavored mustard vinaigrette.

INGREDIENTS

4 slices bacon

3 Tbsp minced red onion

4 Tbsp (2 fl oz/60 ml) extra-virgin olive oil

1½ Tbsp red wine vinegar

½ tsp Dijon mustard

Salt and freshly ground pepper

2 lb (1 kg) green beans, ends trimmed

TOOLS

chef's knife, paring knife, 2 frying pans, small mixing bowl, pot, colander

In a frying pan over medium-high heat, fry the bacon until crisp, about 5 minutes. Transfer to a paper towel–lined plate to drain. Pour off all but 1 tablespoon of the fat from the pan.

Return the pan with the fat to medium heat. Add the onion and sauté until soft, 1–2 minutes. Transfer to a small bowl and stir in 2 tablespoons of the olive oil, the vinegar, the mustard, salt to taste, and 1 teaspoon pepper to make a vinaigrette. Set aside.

Bring a pot full of salted water to a boil over high heat. Add the green beans, reduce the heat to medium-high, and cook until the beans are just tender, 5–7 minutes. Drain, rinse under cold running water, and wrap in a kitchen towel to dry.

In another frying pan over medium-high heat, warm the remaining 2 tablespoons olive oil. When the oil is hot, add the beans and sauté until hot, 3–4 minutes. Remove from the heat and stir in the vinaigrette.

Transfer to a serving bowl or platter, crumble the bacon over the top, and serve.

SERVES 8

APPLE, CELERY, AND SOURDOUGH
BREAD STUFFING

The sweet-tart character of Granny Smith apples combines deliciously with the mild sourness of the bread in this moist, flavorful stuffing. Leaving the crust on the bread adds a nice chewiness, but you can cut it off, if you prefer. We like this stuffing because it is not as rich and filling as many other traditional holiday stuffings.

INGREDIENTS

12 Tbsp (6 oz/185 g) butter, plus more for dish

1 loaf sourdough bread, about 1 lb (500 g)

2 large yellow onions, finely chopped

1½ cups (9 oz/280 g) finely chopped celery, including some leafy tops

2 large Granny Smith apples, halved, cored, and diced

2 Tbsp chopped fresh sage, or 1 tsp dried sage

1 tsp dried thyme

½ tsp freshly grated nutmeg

Salt and freshly ground pepper

⅓ cup (½ oz/15 g) minced fresh flat-leaf parsley

3 large eggs, lightly beaten

2½ cups (20 fl oz/ 625 ml) chicken broth

TOOLS

chef's knife, serrated bread knife, nutmeg grater or rasp grater, assorted mixing bowls, 2 rimmed baking sheets, large frying pan, whisk, 4-qt (4-l) baking dish

Preheat the oven to 250°F (120°C). Lightly butter a 4-qt (4-l) baking dish.

Cut the bread into ½-inch (12-mm) cubes, leaving the crust intact. You should have about 10 cups. Spread the bread cubes on 2 rimmed baking sheets and dry in the oven for 40 minutes. Remove from the oven and set aside. Raise the oven temperature to 375°F (190°C).

In a large frying pan over medium heat, melt 3 tablespoons of the butter. Add the onions and celery and sauté until soft, about 10 minutes. Transfer to a large bowl. Return the pan to medium heat and melt 2 tablespoons more of the butter. Add the apples and sauté until glazed, about 5 minutes. Transfer to the bowl holding the onion-celery mixture. Add the sage, thyme, nutmeg, a big pinch of salt, and ½ teaspoon pepper to the bowl and mix well. Return the pan to medium heat and melt the remaining 7 tablespoons (3½ oz/105 g) butter. Add the bread cubes and parsley and toss to coat. Transfer to the bowl. In another bowl, whisk together the eggs and broth until blended. Pour the broth mixture over the bread mixture and toss gently.

Transfer the stuffing to the prepared baking dish, cover tightly with foil, and bake for 30 minutes. Uncover and continue to bake until the stuffing is hot throughout and lightly browned and crisp on top, 20–30 minutes longer. Serve right away.

SERVES 8–10

BROWN SUGAR PUMPKIN PIE
WITH TOASTED PECAN CRUST

Moist, molasses-rich dark brown sugar and tangy buttermilk add depth to an otherwise traditional pumpkin pie filling. The dough for the cookielike press-in crust is easily made by beating together toasted pecans, butter, flour, egg, and sugar. The result is a homey dessert that fits nicely on nearly any holiday menu.

INGREDIENTS

FOR THE CRUST

½ cup (2 oz/60 g) pecan halves

½ cup (4 oz/125 g) butter, at room temperature

⅓ cup (3 oz/90 g) granulated sugar

1 large egg yolk

½ tsp salt

1¼ cups (6½ oz/200 g) all-purpose flour, plus more for dusting

FOR THE FILLING

1 cup (7 oz/220 g) firmly packed dark brown sugar

2 tsp ground cinnamon

2 tsp ground ginger

1 tsp freshly grated nutmeg

½ tsp salt

¼ tsp ground cloves

1 can (15 oz/470 g) pumpkin purée

¾ cup (6 fl oz/180 ml) buttermilk

4 large eggs

Sweetened whipped cream for serving

TOOLS

nutmeg grater or rasp grater, mixing bowl and whisk or electric mixer, 2 rimmed baking sheets, food processor, large mixing bowl, wooden spoon or electric mixer, 9-inch (23-cm) pie dish, wire rack

Position a rack in the lower third of the oven and another rack in the middle, and preheat to 350°F (180°C).

To make the crust, spread the pecans on a rimmed baking sheet and toast on the middle rack until fragrant and lightly browned, 5–6 minutes. Pour onto a small plate to cool, then pulse until finely ground in a food processor.

In a large bowl, using a wooden spoon or an electric mixer, cream the butter and granulated sugar until thoroughly blended. Beat in the egg yolk and salt. Add the ground pecans and flour and stir until the dough comes together in large, shaggy clumps.

On a lightly floured work surface, press the dough into a mound and knead until it just comes together. Press the dough into a flat disk, then transfer to a 9-inch (23-cm) pie dish. Press the dough evenly into the bottom and up the sides of the dish, dipping your fingers in flour if the dough is sticky. Crimp the edges with the tines of a fork, then freeze the pie shell for 30 minutes.

Meanwhile, to make the filling, combine the brown sugar, cinnamon, ginger, nutmeg, salt, and cloves in the food processor and process until smooth. Add the pumpkin purée, buttermilk, and eggs and process until smooth.

Place the chilled pie shell on a rimmed baking sheet. Pour the filling into the shell and bake on the middle oven rack for 30 minutes. Remove the pie dish from the baking sheet and place it directly on the lower oven rack. Bake until the center of the pie jiggles only slightly when the dish is tapped, 15–20 minutes longer. Let cool completely on a wire rack.

To serve, cut into wedges and top with the whipped cream.

SERVES 8

SPICY GINGERBREAD WITH CREAM CHEESE FROSTING

Traditional warm spices—ginger, cinnamon, cloves—combine with both cayenne and black pepper to give this gingerbread a big, bold character. A crown of fluffy cream-cheese frosting balances the spiciness of the cake. You can make the cake up to two weeks in advance, freeze it, and then move it to the refrigerator to thaw the day before your holiday dinner. Ice the cake just before serving.

INGREDIENTS

½ cup (4 oz/125 g) butter, melted, plus more for dish

2 cups (10 oz/315 g) all-purpose flour

1 Tbsp ground ginger

1½ tsp ground cinnamon

½ tsp ground cloves

½ tsp finely ground black pepper

⅛ tsp cayenne pepper

¾ tsp salt

½ tsp baking powder

½ tsp baking soda

2 large eggs

1 cup (7 oz/220 g) firmly packed light brown sugar

⅔ cup (7½ oz/235 g) dark molasses

1 cup (8 fl oz/250 ml) whole milk

4-inch (10-cm) piece fresh ginger, peeled and grated

FOR THE CREAM CHEESE FROSTING

½ lb (250 g) cream cheese, at room temperature

4 Tbsp (2 oz/60 g) butter, at room temperature

Pinch of salt

⅔ cup (2½ oz/75 g) confectioners' sugar, sifted

1 tsp dry sherry

TOOLS

paring knife, rasp grater, sifter, 8-inch (20-cm) square baking dish, 2 mixing bowls, whisk, silicone spatula, toothpick, wire rack, electric mixer, icing spatula

Preheat the oven to 350°F (180°C). Butter an 8-inch (20-cm) square baking dish.

In a bowl, whisk together the flour, ground ginger, cinnamon, cloves, black pepper, cayenne, salt, baking powder, and baking soda.

In another bowl, whisk the eggs until blended, then add the brown sugar and whisk vigorously to combine. Whisk in the molasses and milk. Add the grated fresh ginger and whisk well.

Pour the egg mixture into the bowl with the flour mixture and stir with a silicone spatula a few times to moisten the ingredients. While stirring, drizzle in the melted butter, mixing just until blended.

Scrape the batter into the prepared baking dish and spread it evenly. Bake until the center springs back when pressed lightly with a fingertip and a toothpick inserted into the center comes out clean, about 40 minutes. Let cool to room temperature in the pan on a wire rack.

While the cake is cooling, make the frosting. Using an electric mixer on medium-high speed, beat together the cream cheese, butter, and salt until light and creamy, 1–2 minutes. Add the confectioners' sugar and beat until smooth. Mix in the sherry.

Using an icing spatula, spread the frosting on the cooled cake. Cut the cake into squares and serve.

SERVES 8–10

FIG COMPOTE WITH HONEY
CRÈME FRAÎCHE

Crème fraîche whips up into a light and fluffy topping for desserts. Here, it is mixed with honey and vanilla for spooning over ripe figs that have been steeped in a red-wine syrup. Store any leftover crème fraîche topping, well covered, in the refrigerator for up to several days, then whisk briefly to rethicken before using.

INGREDIENTS

1 lb (500 g) Black Mission figs, stemmed and halved or quartered lengthwise

¾ cup (6 fl oz/180 ml) dry red wine

¼ cup (2 fl oz/60 ml) fresh orange juice

¼ cup (2 oz/60 g) sugar

½ vanilla bean, split lengthwise

1 cup (8 oz/250 g) crème fraîche

3 Tbsp honey

¼ tsp vanilla extract

TOOLS

paring knife, chef's knife, citrus reamer or press, heatproof mixing bowl, small saucepan, mixing bowl, electric mixer

Put the figs in a heatproof bowl.

In a small saucepan, combine the wine, orange juice, and sugar. Using the tip of a paring knife, scrape the vanilla seeds into the pan. Place over medium heat and bring to a boil, stirring to dissolve the sugar. Boil until the mixture has thickened slightly and is reduced to ¾ cup (6 fl oz/180 ml), about 5 minutes. Pour over the figs and let stand at room temperature until cool.

In a bowl, using an electric mixer on high speed, beat together the crème fraîche, honey, and vanilla extract until thick.

Spoon the fig compote into dessert glasses, top with a dollop of the sweetened crème fraîche, and serve.

SERVES 6

APPLE-CRANBERRY GALETTE

This beautiful open-faced pastry, with scarlet cranberries nestled among golden apple slices, is a gorgeous finale for a holiday meal. Because the fruit filling has been simmered before it goes into the oven, the galette bakes quickly and evenly. This recipe makes 2 galettes—each one will serve 5 or 6 people.

INGREDIENTS

FOR THE PASTRY

1¾ cups (9 oz/280 g) all-purpose flour

6 Tbsp (2 oz/60 g) white cornmeal

2 tsp sugar

¾ tsp salt

¾ cup (6 oz/185 g) cold butter, cut into ½-inch (12-mm) chunks

6 Tbsp (3 oz/90 g) sour cream

½ cup (4 fl oz/125 ml) ice-cold water

FOR THE FILLING

½ cup (4 oz/125 g) sugar

3 Tbsp honey

3 Tbsp fresh lemon juice

½ tsp ground cinnamon

8 large Granny Smith apples, about 4 lb (2 kg) total weight, peeled, cored, and sliced

1½ cups (6 oz/185 g) fresh cranberries

2 Tbsp butter, cut into thin slices

Sugar for dusting (optional)

Crème fraîche for serving (optional)

TOOLS

chef's knife, citrus reamer or press, food processor, assorted mixing bowls, whisk, large frying pan, slotted spoon, rolling pin, 2 baking sheets, 2 wire racks

To make the pastry, combine the flour, cornmeal, sugar, and salt in a food processor. Scatter the chunks of butter over the top and pulse for a few seconds until the butter pieces are the size of small peas. In a small bowl, whisk together the sour cream and ice water. Drizzle the mixture over the dough and pulse until the dough is smooth and clings together. Pat the dough into a disk, wrap in plastic wrap, and refrigerate for 20 minutes.

Meanwhile, to make the filling, in a large frying pan over medium heat, combine the sugar, ½ cup (4 fl oz/125 ml) water, the honey, lemon juice, and cinnamon and cook, stirring, until the sugar dissolves. Stir in the apple slices and simmer until the apples begin to soften, 5–7 minutes. Using a slotted spoon, transfer the apple slices to a bowl. Add the cranberries to the liquid in the frying pan and simmer until they start to pop, about 2 minutes. Using a slotted spoon, add the cranberries to the apples. Boil the liquid over medium-high heat until reduced slightly, and spoon over the fruit.

Position 2 racks in the middle of the oven and preheat to 400°F (200°C).

Divide the dough in half. On a lightly floured work surface, roll out each half into a round about 12 inches (30 cm) in diameter, and transfer to 2 baking sheets. Divide the fruit filling equally between the pastry rounds and spread it in an even layer, leaving a 1½-inch (4-cm) border uncovered. Fold the border over the fruit, pleating the edges to form a rim. Lay the butter slices over the exposed fruit. Dust the pastry rim with sugar, if desired.

Bake the galettes, rotating them 180 degrees at the midway point, until the pastry is golden brown and the apples are tender, 35–40 minutes. Let cool completely on the pans on wire racks before serving. Serve with crème fraîche, if desired.

SERVES 10–12

WINE AND BEER GUIDE

Whether opening a special bottle of wine for an anniversary or holiday, or selecting which beer to serve at a casual dinner, these two beverages are made for food. Here are a few practical tips and pairing suggestions to keep in mind.

The primary role of wine is to make food taste better. Even though we might enjoy a glass by itself or while we're cooking, we both believe that wine's place is alongside food. Now, you don't have to start a wine collection or ever even care about aging a bottle in your house, but it is a good idea to keep at least six bottles on hand. Just keep the wines out of bright sunlight and at an even temperature somewhere below 70°F (20°C) degrees, if you can. They'll last a fairly long time, two to ten years for most reds and two or three years for most whites. If you want to keep a selection of wines in your house, see our recommendations on page 238, along with some pairing tips.

Some convincing arguments can be made that beer often goes better with food than does wine. And it definitely goes better with a day of hot yard work or after a long run in the sun. We usually keep a couple of different kinds of beer around. First, you want a type on hand that is watery and gulpable, like a light Mexican beer or other sippable lagers or pilsners. There's just no substitute for their thirst-quenching drinkability. But we usually keep another style around too, something denser and more complex, which could be anything from a summery Belgian saison-style ale to a hoppy IPA to an English stout. These beers can be drunk warmer and even in wineglasses to appreciate their capacious, exotic aromas.

Here are a few great bites to have with beer:

SAUSAGES AND OTHER CURED MEATS The Germans and Czechs taught us this pairing, and it never goes out of style, especially with a dollop of good mustard.

SHARP-FLAVORED CHEESES Types like Cheddar and Colby go wonderfully with bitter, hop-charged beers like IPA that can sometimes be difficult to pair with food.

NUTTY-FLAVORED CHEESES Cave-aged Gruyère, Comté, and Gouda are lovely paired with malty amber and nut brown ales.

SEAFOOD Whether it's boiled shrimp and cocktail sauce, cracked crab, or oysters on the half shell, almost all crustaceans make a great match with pilsners and moderately hoppy ales.

THE MINI HOME WINE CELLAR

Champagne or other sparkling wine. You never know when you might need it to celebrate—perhaps every day?

Crisp, refreshing whites. Keep on hand a bottle each of Sauvignon Blanc (New Zealand or France) and Riesling (Germany, Austria, or Alsace).

Richer whites. Stock two bottles of Chardonnay (France or California), good by themselves or with rich foods.

Light reds. Beaujolais and Pinot Noir, are easy to drink by themselves or with poultry and meats.

Medium-bodied reds. Chianti, Rioja, and Montepulciano are some of our favorites for weeknight meals, pizza suppers, and the like.

Full-bodied reds. Break out the big guns— Cabernet Sauvignon (Napa or Bordeaux), Malbec (Argentina), or Shiraz (Australia)—when serving steaks, stews, roasts, and chops.

Sweet wine. We like Port or Madeira. The latter is especially delicious with desserts and cheeses, and will last open without degrading for years.

THE TRUTH ABOUT WINEGLASSES

Yes, you need good wineglasses. Just as music doesn't sound good through tinny speakers, bad glasses do no favors to good wines. That said, you don't need a different glass for every varietal. Here's how to fill out your collection, and enjoy it well.

BURGUNDY GLASSES These have rounder, broader bowls and slightly shorter stems than a standard red-wine glass, to allow bold flavors and aromas to breathe. They are good for Pinot Noir, Chardonnay, or Italian reds from Nebbiolo or Sangiovese grapes.

STANDARD RED-WINE GLASSES These don't have to be huge, just wide enough to swirl and wider at the top than the Burgundy glass. Drink all other red wines from these glasses.

SMALL WHITE-WINE GLASSES These versatile wineglasses should be daintier and more U shaped than the glasses for reds. These are good for aromatic whites like Sauvignon Blanc and Riesling, and even for Champagne, which tastes best in a white-wine glass.

DESSERT-WINE GLASSES These are the smallest of the wineglasses, portioned to hold a few sweet sips to finish the meal. Bring them out with dessert to enjoy late-harvest wines such as Muscat and Sauternes. You can use small white-wine glasses in their place.

STEMLESS GLASSES For casual gatherings, stemless glasses are both attractive and functional. If you're chatting and sipping in the kitchen, you'll find them less prone to toppling over. Filled with a summery rosé, they are just right for an outdoor party.

PARTY GLASSES Champagne flutes look festive, and their tall shape helps trap air bubbles, enhancing the wine's effervescence. And as to the rest of the bar: use stemmed glasses with V-shaped bowls for any mixed drink served without ice; martini glasses for martinis, cosmopolitans, and blender drinks; and tumblers and straight-sided highball glasses for mixed drinks and soft drinks.

GET CRYSTAL Riedel, Schott Zwiesel, and Spiegelau are all good brands. You want a very thin lip on the glass, as the graceful delivery of the wine onto the tongue is key.

HOLD YOUR WINEGLASS BY ITS STEM A lot of people pick the glass up by the bowl, but in the wine world, that's bad form—it raises the temperature of the wine and leaves unsightly fingerprints.

KEEP GLASSES SPARKLING CLEAN You can wash glasses in the dishwasher. If you opt to do it by hand, the only parts of the glass that get dirty and require soap are the rim, the outside of the bowl, and the stem. Be gentle and dry upside down on a towel.

ELEMENTS OF THE TABLE

Setting the table can be as involved or as relaxed as you want it to be. Below you'll find the traditional approach to formal place settings, but feel free to adjust per your personal style and the occasion, or opt for family-style serving. The object remains the same: place the elements within easy reach and create a welcoming table.

LINENS A simple, neutral tablecloth is suitable for any occasion. But think of linens, including a runner, placemats, and napkins, as an expressive way to change the look of your table from season to season; to add color; or to dress it up for special occasions. Place a folded napkin to the left of the forks, its folded side facing the plate, ready to be unfurled as guests sit down.

PLATES At the center of each setting, stack the plates by order of use. For formal occasions, place a charger, also known as the service plate, first. Purely decorative (no food is served on it), a charger can add color and interest to the table. Next is the dinner plate, a large plate used for the main course and side dishes. On top goes the salad plate. Set a small plate for bread, if using, just above the forks.

CUTLERY In general, cutlery is arranged by order of use starting from the outside in. Forks are placed to the left of the plate. The salad fork is typically placed furthest left (although this indicates that salad will be served first; if serving salad after the main course, place the fork accordingly). At center is the dinner fork; used for the main course, this is the largest fork in the setting. The dessert fork is set nearest to the dinner plate, but, if you prefer, you can bring out the dessert forks with coffee and dessert.

Knives and spoons are arranged to the right of the dinner plate. The sturdy table knife is set to the right of the plate, its blade facing inward. If you are serving steaks, chops, or roasted meat, you can replace the table knife with a steak knife.

Place a teaspoon to the right of the table knife. Or, you can bring out the teaspoons at the same time you bring out coffee. If serving soup, place a soupspoon to the right of the teaspoon or knife.

Lay a small butter knife on the bread plate, if using.

GLASSES Set a tumbler or goblet for water just above the knife. Fill water glasses before the guests are seated. To the right and slightly above the water glass, set the wineglass for the first wine being served (usually a white). For each additional wine you plan to pour, place another wineglass to the right of the previous one on a slight diagonal.

EXTRA TOUCHES Lighting, music, and flowers all help to set the mood and create ambiance. Choose votives or tall tapers, but stick with unscented candles, which won't compete with the aromas of the food. Choose bouquets and centerpieces of moderate size, so they won't block the view from across the table.

PLACE CARDS They may be an old-fashioned tradition, but done well, seating arrangements encourage conversation and put your guests at ease. You can direct guests as they sit down, or you can place small name cards at each setting. Simple pieces of card stock with written or printed names are fine, but you can be as creative as you like with other materials.

KITCHEN ESSENTIALS

If your wedding was at all like ours, you probably got a lot of loot—some fantastic, some less so. It's funny how we got some things that we wanted but have yet to use, and others, like a panini press, that we didn't ask for and have grown to love. That said, there is some equipment that every kitchen should have. Invest in quality essentials, and you'll have all that you need to pull off meals, from the simple to the spectacular.

COOKWARE, BAKEWARE, AND ELECTRICS

☐ **DUTCH OVEN**
A sturdy cast-iron pot, such as Le Creuset, works equally well on the stove top and in the oven.

☐ **FRYING PANS**
One nonstick, one regular (preferably stainless steel with an aluminum or copper core for good heat conduction), and one cast iron. Aim for different sizes. You'll also need sauté pans with lids, one large and one small, for poaching eggs, braising, and, of course, sautéing.

☐ **GRILL PAN**
A stove-top grill pan is a handy alternative for recipes that call for charcoal or gas grilling.

☐ **ROASTING PAN**
A large, heavy-duty rectangular pan for cooking big items (like the Thanksgiving turkey).

☐ **SAUCEPANS**
You need at least three: small, medium, and large.

☐ **STOCKPOT**
Besides making stock, this tall, narrow pot is good for boiling pasta, lobster, and other foods that require a large amount of water.

☐ **BAKING DISHES**
One rectangular and one square dish in glass or ceramic are a good start. Popular sizes are 9-by-13-inches (23-by-33-cm) and 8-inches (20-cm) square. We use a 9-inch (23-cm) square baking pan for lasagne (page 161) and granita (page 145).

☐ **BAKING SHEETS**
At least two, a rimless sheet for baking cookies and pastries, and a rimmed sheet for broiling and roasting vegetables and other uses.

☐ **CAKE PANS**
Two round 8- or 9-inch (20- or 23-cm) heavy metal pans for when you want to make a layer cake.

☐ **PIE DISH**
Our 9-inch (23-cm) ceramic dish is stylish enough to go from the oven to the table. It's also deeper, and thus holds more filling, than most metal pie pans.

☐ **TART PAN**
Look for a 10- or 11-inch (25- or 28-cm) pan with a removable bottom and fluted sides for making pretty French-inspired tarts.

☐ **MUFFIN PAN**
A standard 12-cup pan does double duty for cupcakes and muffins.

☐ **BLENDERS**
It is good to have two types, a canister blender and an immersion blender. The former is great for mixing smoothies, milk shakes, and cocktails. The latter is handy for blending soups right in the pot.

☐ **HANDHELD MIXER**
A small, light handheld mixer works just fine for batters and most soft doughs and for beating egg whites and cream.

☐ **FOOD PROCESSOR**
This machine and its attachments does so many things—mixes, chops, purées, shreds, grates, kneads—that you don't want to live without one.

☐ **COFFEE GRINDER**
Yes, a coffee grinder is essential. Coffee made from the preground stuff just isn't as good.

☐ **TOASTER OVEN**
You can do so much with a toaster oven, like melt cheese, reheat sandwiches, and toast nuts.

TOOLS

☐ **MIXING BOWLS**
We use our set of six stainless-steel bowls for all
of our mixing needs. They are light, durable, and,
like Russian dolls, stack snugly inside one another.

☐ **COLANDER AND SIEVE**
One colander, for draining pasta and vegetables,
and one fine-mesh sieve for everything else.

☐ **KNIVES**
Two chef's knives, 8 inches (20 cm) and 11 inches
(28 cm), made of carbon steel or a carbon–stainless
steel alloy for easy sharpening; one or two paring
knives; a long serrated knife for slicing bread; and
a honing steel or other sharpener for keeping your
knives in good working order.

☐ **GRATERS**
A box grater-shredder for large vegetables, and a
rasp-type grater for citrus zests, ginger, and cheese.

☐ **VEGETABLE PEELER**
A swivel-bladed peeler for peeling vegetables
and fruits and for shaving cheeses and chocolate.

☐ **MORTAR AND PESTLE**
Ideal for crushing, grinding, or blending small
amounts. Ours is made of marble.

☐ **SPOONS, SPATULAS, AND LADLES**
Assorted wooden spoons; silicone spatulas for
blending and cooking; a large slotted metal spoon
for removing solids from liquids; a metal spatula
for turning pancakes or fish fillets; and a ladle for
soups, stews, and batters.

☐ **WHISKS**
One large and one small.

☐ **TONGS**
Two pairs of hinged stainless-steel tongs for
grasping or turning foods without piercing them.

☐ **FLAT MEAT POUNDER**
This flat metal disk with a handle makes quick work
of flattening boneless meat to an even thickness.

☐ **SHEARS**
A pair of sturdy shears for cutting everything
from herbs to parchment paper, and a pair of
poultry shears for getting through joints and
around bones.

☐ **MEASURING CUPS AND SPOONS**
One or two glass measuring cups for liquids (one
with a 2-cup/16 fl oz/500 ml capacity); a set of dry
measuring cups; and a set of spoons.

☐ **BRUSHES**
A sturdy-bristled brush for scrubbing vegetables
and two fine-bristled pastry brushes, one for savory
tasks and one for sweet.

☐ **ROLLING PIN**
Choose one that's heavy and well made.

☐ **CITRUS REAMER OR PRESS**
Either will work. A reamer is just a conical ribbed
blade with a handle. If you opt for the press, choose
one that is large enough to squeeze an orange, and
it will work for lemons and limes, too.

☐ **PEPPER GRINDER**
Get a big, high-quality grinder that lets you adjust
the coarseness of the grind.

☐ **THERMOMETERS**
An instant-read thermometer for checking the
doneness of meat, poultry, and fish, and a deep-
frying and candy thermometer for testing oil and
sugar syrups.

☐ **WOODEN CUTTING BOARDS**
You need two boards, one for meat, poultry, and
seafood and one for vegetables, fruits, and other
items. A carving board, with a groove around the
perimeter for capturing juices, is also nice to have.

☐ **WIRE RACKS**
For cooling cakes, pies, cookies, and just about
anything else that needs cooling.

☐ **STEAMER BASKET**
A collapsible metal basket that fits into different-
sized pans.

☐ **SALAD SPINNER**
Eliminates all worries about wet lettuce leaves
in your salads.

☐ **CORKSCREW**
A no-frills waiter's corkscrew is all you need.

☐ **POTATO MASHER**
Choose one with a heavy wire grid and sturdy handle.

TIPS FOR ORGANIZING YOUR KITCHEN

- An ideal kitchen is both comfortable and funtional. If possible, maintain two separate work areas, each with a cutting board and plenty of counter space, so that two cooks can maneuver easily in the space.

- Even if space is tight we recommend installing some sort of island. When it's not being used to prep ingredients, our butcher-block island adds immeasurably to the kitchen's sociability.

- We're fans of open shelves, or even of taking the doors off of some cupboards, to showcase your kitchen equipment and make it more accessible.

- Things to keep within easy reach: mixing bowls, knives, wooden spoons, plates.

- Put pots and pans that get the most use close to the stove. If your kitchen is small and your ceiling can support a rack, hang them to free up space and add a cozy feeling.

- Keep cutting boards near the sink to make washing them after each use easy.

- We keep our wooden spoons in a crock next to the stove, and we keep them separate from the metal ones because we like the way it looks.

- Don't store your knives carelessly, or you risk injury to your hands and dull or nicked blades. Use a countertop knife block or a drawer storage tray.

- Good lighting is essential, especially above the stove. If the room lighting isn't sufficient, consider installing a light directly over the stove.

- Keep a collapsible stepladder on hand, tucked into a corner or closet, for fetching things off of high shelves (it's much easier than dragging a chair from the dining room).

OUR PANTRY ESSENTIALS

- Pasta (four kinds, fettuccine, spaghetti, penne, and couscous)
- Canned tomatoes and tomato paste
- Canned tuna, canned clams, and canned or jarred anchovy fillets
- Dried and canned beans (black, white, chickpeas)
- Rice (white and brown)
- Grains (quinoa, farro)
- All-purpose flour, baking powder, and baking soda
- Sugar (granulated, brown, and superfine)
- Salt (kosher, sea) and peppercorns
- Capers, olives, and pickles
- Worcestershire sauce, soy sauce, and mustards
- A mix of oils (see note at right)
- Vinegar (white wine, red wine, and cider)
- Onions and garlic

STOCKING YOUR PANTRY

The pantry is the most interesting part of the kitchen, and we tend ours like our mothers tend their gardens: constantly weeding out old ingredients and clutter and planting new, delectable items on the shelves.

You might think that pantries are only for staples like flour, sugar, and oatmeal and are wondering how that can be interesting. But the best pantries are home to much more than everyday items. Ours harbors unusual aromatic spices picked up on a trip to Europe, gourmet canned goods like San Marzano tomatoes and olive oil–packed tuna, and such flavor enhancers as Madagascar vanilla beans, salt-packed capers, balsamic vinegar, and bonito flakes. Pantries also hold such important complements to main courses as quinoa, white beans, farro, and couscous.

Finally, when you're hungry but don't have anything fresh in the fridge to cook, creating a pantry meal, sourced entirely from stuff that you have on hand, can lead to memorably good and creative dishes like white bean salad, fried rice, or pasta with tomatoes, olives, and canned tuna. Some of our most satisfying meals have been just that, put together after a day of hiking or an evening at a party.

So stock your pantry well and you'll always be prepared. Not only will its contents come in handy in a pinch, but you might also find a culinary treasure on the shelf that can help transform a dish from good to great.

A NOTE ABOUT OILS

You'll want to have a few different types of oil in your pantry or cupboard, stored away from light. We keep olive oil on hand for cooking, as well as one high-quality extra-virgin olive oil for finishing. We always stock canola or other neutral oil, such as grapeseed, and a nice nut oil, such as walnut or hazelnut, for making salad dressings.

SEASONING WITH HERBS AND SPICES

In most of our cooking, we don't go crazy with spices and herbs for fear of overwhelming the taste of quality ingredients. We always like to have a few around, however. Here's what we generally have on hand, for fresh and dried herbs, as well as spices.

BASIL A basil plant is fussier than a parsley plant, but if you can keep it alive, you'll always have something to go with tomatoes.

BLACK PEPPERCORNS You'll want a grinder that has two settings, one for fine grind and one for coarse grind.

CARDAMOM This fragrant, sweet spice is delicious in everything from stews to cookies to cocktails.

CHILE POWDER A good way to add an earthy flavor to meat and vegetable dishes.

CUMIN This goes into big pots of black beans, which we make almost every week.

CURRY POWDER One of our favorite spices for flavoring a great one-dish supper.

DILL We like the delicate, sweet flavor of both fresh and dried dill in light salad dressings.

FENNEL SEEDS These aromatic seeds are great for adding high tones to a ragù or a meat rub.

FLAT-LEAF PARSLEY It's easy to keep a plant growing indoors, and handy for that little garnish every cook needs.

MINT Our mint plant does double duty, yielding leaves for seasoning dishes, especially fruit salads and lamb, and for making a lovely after-dinner tisane.

OREGANO We add small doses of this pungent, dried herb to ragù.

ROSEMARY The bush we planted in our front yard is thriving and we clip sprigs often.

SALT Keep a small bowl of kosher salt on hand for seasoning while you're cooking (it is easier to pinch between fingertips and dissolves more quickly than other salts) and keep a larger container of sea salt for brining and for seasoning pasta and vegetable water.

THYME Easy to grow, thyme is our go-to seasoning for poultry.

TIPS FOR THE FREEZER

We see the freezer as an extension of the pantry, good for quick meals if you didn't have a chance to go shopping that day.

Keep it well stocked. Our freezer always holds one free-range chicken, a couple of steaks, some sausages, frozen fruits (for smoothies), chicken stock, peas, and a loaf of sliced bread.

Label, label, label. We always tape a Post-it note on the package that identifies the contents and the date it went into the freezer. Freezing is a great way to preserve all kinds of foods, but after a while in the deep cold, foods lose flavor and texture, so check the dates often.

Double bag or vacuum seal items. Protecting foods from freezer burn and oxidation is paramount, so wrap everything well.

BASIC RECIPES

The recipes that follow serve as building blocks for many meals. Although some of these items can be purchased for convenience, you'll find that your homemade dishes taste even better if you make these elements yourself. Some can be made ahead, perhaps on a quiet weekend day when you have some free time to devote to cooking, and refrigerated or frozen until needed.

CHICKEN STOCK

5 lb (2½ kg) chicken backs and necks

1 yellow onion, quartered

2 carrots, peeled and cut in half

1 rib celery, cut in half

2 sprigs fresh flat-leaf parsley

1 sprig fresh thyme

1 bay leaf

Combine the chicken parts with 4 qt (4 l) water in a large stockpot and bring to a boil. Reduce the heat to low and use a large spoon to skim off any gray foam that rises to the surface. (Do not skim off the fat, however, as this locks in flavor as the stock cooks.) Add the onion, carrots, celery, parsley, thyme, and bay leaf, reduce the heat to low, and simmer gently, uncovered, until the stock tastes rich and is a light golden color, about 3 hours. Strain the stock through a fine-mesh sieve and let cool completely. Skim off any fat from the surface. Use immediately or cover and refrigerate for up to 3 days (remove the hardened white fat from the surface after chilling) or freeze for up to 6 months.

MAKES ABOUT 3 QUARTS (3 L)

BEEF STOCK

6 lb (3 kg) meaty beef shanks and knuckles

3 carrots, peeled and cut in half

2 yellow onions, quartered

3 ribs celery, cut in half

4 sprigs fresh flat-leaf parsley

2 sprigs fresh thyme

½ bay leaf

5 whole black peppercorns

Preheat the oven to 425°F (220°C). Arrange the beef shanks and knuckles in a heavy roasting pan and roast, turning once, until thoroughly browned, 20–25 minutes. Combine the roasted bones with 5 qt (5 l) water in a large stockpot and bring to a boil.

Meanwhile, place the roasting pan with the drippings over 2 burners and turn the heat to medium-high. Add ⅓ cup (3 fl oz/80 ml) water to the roasting pan and bring to a brisk simmer. Deglaze the pan, stirring and scraping with a wooden spoon to loosen the browned bits from the bottom. Add the flavorful pan drippings to the pot.

When the stock reaches a boil, use a large spoon to skim off any gray foam that rises to the surface. Add the carrots, onions, celery, parsley, thyme, bay leaf, and peppercorns, reduce the heat to low, and simmer gently, uncovered, until the stock tastes rich and is a light caramel color, about 5 hours. Strain the stock through a fine-mesh sieve and let cool completely. Skim off any fat from the surface. Use immediately or cover and refrigerate for up to 3 days (remove the hardened white fat from the surface after chilling) or freeze for up to 6 months.

MAKES ABOUT 3 QUARTS (3 L)

VEGETABLE STOCK

2 yellow onions, thickly sliced

1 leek, rinsed and thickly sliced

2 carrots, peeled and coarsely chopped

2 ribs celery, coarsely chopped

4 sprigs fresh flat-leaf parsley

6 whole black peppercorns

1 bay leaf

2 sprigs fresh thyme

Combine all the ingredients with 4 qt (4 l) water in a large stockpot and bring to a boil. Reduce the heat to low and simmer gently, uncovered, for 1 hour. Strain the stock through a fine-mesh sieve, pressing on the vegetables with the back of a spoon to extract as much liquid as possible. Discard the vegetables. Use the stock immediately, or cover and refrigerate for up to 3 days or freeze for up to 6 months.

MAKES ABOUT 3½ QUARTS (3½ L)

PIZZA DOUGH

2¾ cups (14 oz/440 g) bread flour, plus more for dusting

¼ cup (1½ oz/45 g) semolina flour

2 tsp rapid-rise yeast

1½ tsp fine sea salt

3 Tbsp extra-virgin olive oil, plus more for greasing

In a food processor, combine the bread flour and semolina flour, the yeast, and the salt and pulse briefly to mix. With the motor running, drizzle in 1 cup (8 fl oz/ 250 ml) water and then the oil. Process just until a ball of dough forms.

Turn the dough out onto a lightly floured work surface and knead until smooth and elastic, 2–3 minutes. Pat back into a ball.

Lightly oil a large bowl. Put the ball of dough in the bowl and turn to coat with the oil. Cover the bowl with plastic wrap and let the dough rise in a warm spot until doubled in bulk, about 1½ hours.

Punch the dough down and knead briefly to remove any air bubbles. Roll out into a round or oval, or as directed in the recipe. If not using immediately, shape into a disk, transfer to a lock-top plastic bag, and refrigerate for up to 1 day or freeze for up to 1 month. Let the dough come to room temperature before using.

MAKES 1½ LB (750 G) DOUGH

PASTA DOUGH

2 cups (10 oz/315 g) unbleached all-purpose flour, plus more as needed

1 Tbsp semolina flour

½ tsp fine sea salt

Pinch of freshly grated nutmeg

3 extra-large eggs, lightly beaten

1–2 Tbsp extra-virgin olive oil

In a food processor, combine the all-purpose flour and semolina flour, salt, and nutmeg and pulse briefly to mix. Add the eggs and process briefly. Drizzle in 1 tablespoon of the olive oil and process until the mixture forms curdlike crumbs. When you pinch the dough it should form a soft ball. If it is too wet or sticky, add more flour, 1 tablespoon at a time, and process briefly. If it is too dry, drizzle in the remaining 1 tablespoon oil.

Turn the dough out onto a lightly floured work surface and knead until smooth and firm but pliable. This will take several minutes. Wrap the dough tightly in plastic wrap and let sit at room temperature for 30 minutes.

To roll out the dough, cut it into 4 equal pieces. Cover 3 pieces with plastic wrap. Briefly knead the fourth piece on a lightly floured surface. Set the rollers of a pasta machine to the widest setting, then crank the dough through the rollers. Fold the dough into thirds and pass it through the rollers again. Repeat folding and rolling two or three times until the dough is smooth. Reset the rollers

one width narrower and crank the dough through the setting twice, then adjust the rollers to the next narrowest setting. Continue to pass the dough through the rollers twice on each setting until you have a long, very thin sheet.

Lay the dough sheet on a lightly floured surface and cut into 4-by-5-inch (10-by-13-cm) rectangles for lasagne, or cut the sheet into noodles as directed in individual recipes. Repeat with the remaining 3 dough portions.

MAKES 1 LB (500 G) DOUGH

TOMATO-BASIL SAUCE

3 Tbsp extra-virgin olive oil

5 cloves garlic, minced

3 lb (1.5 kg) fresh plum tomatoes or 1 can (28 oz/875 g) crushed plum tomatoes

1 bay leaf

2 tsp sugar

Salt and freshly ground pepper

½ cup (1 oz/30 g) firmly packed torn fresh basil leaves

In a large saucepan over medium heat, warm the oil. Add the garlic and cook until it is golden on all sides, about 4 minutes. Remove from the heat.

If using fresh tomatoes, core and quarter them. Working in batches, purée the tomatoes in a blender until smooth, and then strain through a coarse-mesh sieve into the pan with the oil and garlic. If using canned tomatoes, add them to the pan with the oil and garlic. Add the bay leaf, sugar, 1 teaspoon salt, and a few grinds of pepper. Place over medium-high heat and bring to a boil. Reduce the heat to low and simmer, uncovered, until thickened, about 45 minutes. Add the basil and cook for another 5 minutes. Taste and adjust the seasoning with salt and pepper. Use right away, or remove from the heat and let cool slightly if using for lasagne. The sauce can be stored in the refrigerator for up to 1 week or in the freezer for up to 6 months.

MAKES ABOUT 3 CUPS (24 FL OZ/750 ML)

POLENTA

Salt

1 cup (7 oz/220 g) polenta

Bring a pot with 3 cups (24 fl oz/ 750 ml) salted water to a boil over high heat. Gradually pour the polenta into the water, whisking constantly. Reduce the heat to low and cook, stirring constantly, for 10–15 minutes, until the water is absorbed and the polenta is soft. Serve right away, or to make polenta squares, pour into a lightly greased baking pan to a depth of 1½ inches (4 cm). After about 2 hours, cut the cooled polenta into squares and serve.

MAKES 4–6 SERVINGS

FRESH BREAD CRUMBS

4 large slices stale country bread, or 1 stale baguette

Remove the crusts from the bread and discard. Tear the bread into pieces. Put the bread in a food processor and pulse until you have irregular, pea-sized crumbs, or pulse longer for fine crumbs. You can freeze freshly made bread crumbs in a lock-top plastic bag for up to 1 month.

MAKES ABOUT 1 CUP (2 OZ/60 G)

Note: To make toasted bread crumbs, preheat the oven to 325°F (165°C). Toss the fresh bread crumbs with about 1 Tbsp extra-virgin olive oil and a pinch of salt. Spread the crumbs on a baking sheet and bake until crisp and very golden, 12–15 minutes.

HARD-BOILED EGGS

Salt

4 large eggs

Have ready an ice bath. In a saucepan over high heat, bring 1 qt (1 l) salted water to a boil. Lower the eggs gently into the water with a slotted spoon and reduce the heat to a gentle simmer. Exactly 8 minutes after adding the eggs to the water, remove them with the slotted spoon and plunge them into the ice bath to stop the cooking. When cool, after 30 seconds–1 minute, crack and peel the eggs. The shells will peel more easily after the ice bath.

MAKES 4 HARD-BOILED EGGS

MAYONNAISE

1 large egg

1 tsp Dijon mustard

1 tsp lemon juice or white wine vinegar

Kosher salt and freshly ground pepper

¾ cup (6 fl oz/180 ml) vegetable oil

¾ cup (6 fl oz/180 ml) extra-virgin olive oil

Warm the uncracked egg in a bowl of hot tap water for 3 minutes. In a blender or food processor, combine the egg, mustard, lemon juice, 1 teaspoon salt, and ¼ teaspoon pepper. In a bowl, combine the vegetable and olive oils. With the motor running, slowly drizzle the combined oils into the blender (this should take several minutes) to make a thick mayonnaise. Stir in 1 tablespoon hot water.

MAKES 1¾ CUPS (14 FL OZ/430 ML)

CRÈME FRAÎCHE

1 cup (8 fl oz/250 ml) heavy cream

1 Tbsp buttermilk

Combine the cream and buttermilk in a small saucepan and warm over medium-low heat. Do not allow to simmer. Remove the mixture from the heat, cover loosely, and let thicken and sour at warm room temperature until it suits your taste, 8–48 hours. Once it is as thick and flavorful as you want it, chill well before using.

MAKES 1 CUP (8 FL OZ/250 ML)

INDEX